The Topping Book

Or,
Getting Good At Being Bad

The Topping Book

Or,
Getting Good At Being Bad

by Dossie Easton &
Catherine A. Liszt

Illustrated by Fish

Greenery
Press

Published in the United States by Greenery Press, 3739 Balboa
Ave. #195, San Francisco, CA 94121, verdant@crl.com.

ISBN 0-9739763-5-4

Table of Contents

Illustrations are on pages vii, 13, 28, 47, 58, 66, 80, 92, 104, 117, 145 and 156.

Acknowledgements

Our deepest thanks go to the following wonderful people, who have bottomed to us, topped us, given us wonderful ideas and just plain been our friends:

Akasha
Mic Bergen
Tom B.
Bill Brent
Kaye Buckley
Lady Cassandra
Derek
Francesca Guido
Irwin Kane
Ruth Marks
Master Max
Amy Marie Meek
Snow White
Joi Wolfwomyn

And our most profound and heartfelt thanks and love to our partners, Kai Harper and Jay Wiseman, who coached us through our labor pains and were unbelievably understanding about our collaboration and friendship. We couldn't have done it without you.

Chapter 1. Hello Again!

We love tops.

We love tops who are vicious and nasty and turn their bottoms into cringing mounds of adoring submission. We love tops who are nurturing and sweet while they inflict the most amazing agonies. We love tops whose aura of command is so matter-of-fact that their bottoms can completely forget, for a little while, that the world is a complicated place.

We love top daddies and top mommies, top nurses and top interrogators, sweetheart sadists and control queens, nasty kids and mad scientists.

We love tops so much that we're writing a book to help make sure there are more good ones: tops who glow with the pure white light of control, power, intimacy and love; tops who are skilled at their craft and passionate about their art; tops who pour themselves into their bottoms, beat well, and create a dish as fiery as curry or as sweet as pie.

Yes, it's us again. Hello. We're Dossie Easton and Catherine A. Liszt. Some of you met us in our earlier book, "The Bottoming Book: Or, How To Get Terrible Things Done To You By Wonderful People."

Dossie is a two-decade veteran of S/M play who identifies as a dyke queer bottom, but who tops beautifully (as of this writing, Catherine has the cane marks to prove it). She works as a therapist in San Francisco and Marin County. A poet, teacher and performer, Dossie was one of the first members of the Society of Janus in San Francisco, and has been a leader in the S/M spirituality community.

Catherine started doing S/M about a decade ago, exclusively as a heterosexual top. Today, she still identifies as a top, but plays both as a top and as a bottom, and with both men and women. Under her other pen name "Lady Green," she wrote the how-to manual "The Sexually Dominant Woman: A Workbook for Nervous Beginners," and has published many articles on S/M practice and philosophy.

Fish, our illustrator, is a San Francisco artist, journalist and publisher. She has been creating S/M comics and illustrations since 1990, and publishes a great magazine called <u>Brat Attack: The Zine for Leatherdykes and Other Bad Girls</u> (see Resource Guide for ordering information).

Why we're writing this. In "The Bottoming Book," we did our best to explain what makes people decide to try bottoming in an S/M interaction, and the attitudes and techniques that make up a brilliant bottom. We looked at matters of the body, emotions, intuition and spirit.

In this book we will do the same for tops. In some ways, we expect this to be a trickier task. While outsiders often assume that any S/M person in his/her right mind would be a top - "Wow, you mean people will do anything you want them to? Cool!" - the reality is that the joys of topping are often more abstract than those of bottoming, and that its responsibilities and burdens are great. "The Bottoming Book" was, as we wrote in the introduction, "an unabashedly bottom-centrist book." We expected howls of protest from tops over our insistence that bottoms are powerful, beautiful and irreplaceable... and we heard back from a whole bunch of tops saying "Well, it's about *time.*"

So "The Topping Book" will be a *top*-centrist book. While we will, of course, expect responsible behavior from all you tops and wannabe-tops who are reading this, we honor and applaud your willingness to venture out on the thin, scary ice of taking control of another's sensations, emotions and spirit. In this book, we'll encourage you to insist on being recognized for your humanness as well as for your toppiness, to demand the nurturance and support you deserve, and to find ways to get your sexual needs met. We'll do our best to hold your hand during the scary parts of your top journey, and to wave an encouraging bye-bye as you venture out into that wide, welcoming world of eager bottoms.

We don't want to be your first. We're not going to spend a lot of time in this book advising you on bondage knots or clamp placement or the other technical nuts and bolts of topping. We think there are several other good books out there that teach such things, and we've listed them in our Resource Guide. We're also not going to go into a lot of detail about S/M terminology or philosophy.

We're writing this for the player who has a basic sound grasp of the rudiments of S/M. If this is the first S/M book you've ever read, and you don't have a lot of play experience, we're going to ask you to turn to the Resource Guide and order one or two of the excellent introductory books there, or to contact your local S/M club and attend a few programs. Then come back to us - we'll be waiting for you.

How We View S/M

If you turned to this section hoping to find the ultimate incontestable answer to the question "What is S/M?" we're afraid we're going to have to disappoint you. We don't know, either.

We do believe that consensual, ethical S/M has a valid place on the continuum of human sexual behavior - that it's not an expression of pathology. We also do not see S/M players as a distinct sexual minority, somehow different from other folk; we think S/M may be further along one road of sexual exploration, but that many if not most people play with some forms of S/M energy.

S/M is sex that involves all of our faculties: minds and bodies, imagination and intellect, hearts and souls. To those who call S/M "unnatural," we like to point out that we do what comes naturally: nature gave us opposable thumbs, so we use tools.

As we said in "The Bottoming Book": "S/M is play, theater, communication, intimacy, sexuality. It combines the child's urge for make-believe with the adult's ability to take responsibility and the adult's privilege of sexual reward. S/M at its best represents a remarkable convergence of civilized agreements and primitive urges. We believe it to be a very high achievement of the human body, mind and spirit."

Yes, but what _is_ it? We argued for hours as we worked on this book, and we weren't able to come up with a definition that we thought accurately encompassed all of what we know as S/M. Here, though, are some of the definitions we and our friends use and like.

A lot of folks use the phrase "consensual power exchange" to define S/M. We're not entirely happy with this phrase - we think using the word "power," that so often means nonconsensual force and coercion, can be misleading. In fact, what we do in S/M is that we *act as though* we were giving up or taking real-world power, while retaining the ability to keep as much power as we need to feel safe, or to take no more than we feel OK about having.

Catherine's working definition is:

S/M is an activity in which the participants eroticize sensations or emotions that would be unpleasant in a non-erotic context.

We've heard some objections to the word "eroticize" in this definition - not everybody who does S/M connects their activities to genital sexuality. But we prefer to use the word "erotic" to refer to a wide spectrum of emotions and sensations that are arousing, awakening, enlightening and stimulating - whether or not they make your dick hard or your pussy wet.

Our friend Mikey says:

S/M is what happens when the top takes more than the bottom offers, but less than the bottom is willing to give.

We think that this thought does a nice job of expressing the tension that often happens in good S/M - the "oh-my-god-this-is-terrible-please-don't-stop" energy that we all know and love.

Another good thought we've heard is:

S/M takes place when the top trades his or her energy for the bottom's armor.

4

All these definitions convey good information, but none of them seems to us adequate or comprehensive.

One thing we *do* know is that S/M is completely and qualitatively different from abuse. S/M bears the same relationship to abuse that consensual sex does to rape: a photograph of an S/M scene might look exactly like a photo of an abuse incident, but what is going on in the hearts and minds of the participants is entirely different. Hence, we say:

In S/M, the participants have one another's well-being as their paramount goal.

Some folks get confused because the fantasies they use to get turned on are not about consensual S/M. (Ours certainly aren't!) If you feel disturbed by this seeming contradiction, let us remind you: everyone in your fantasy exists only inside your head. Since they are all aspects of yourself, they have all given their consent to be there. One of the characteristics that defines safe S/M is a recognition of the boundaries between our fantasies and our realities. A lot of this book will be devoted to helping clarify those boundaries.

In general, though, we'd say that if it looks like S/M to you, then it's probably S/M - or at least something close enough that you can learn more about it by reading on.

All those different words! As you can see, throughout this book we are using S/M to refer to the broad spectrum of activities and behaviors that fall under the miscellaneous categories of "S/M" (sadomasochism), "B/D" (bondage and discipline), "D/S" (dominance and submission), "leathersex," "fetish" and a bunch of others. We are aware that this terminology is not universal - many folks prefer to use S/M to refer only to activities involving the giving or receiving of strong sensation - but it's the one we're used to, so please hang with us.

Similarly, we will use the word "top" to mean sadists, dominants, masters, mistresses, owners, trainers, teachers, daddies, mommies, interrogators and other active parties - and "bottom" to mean slaves, masochists, submissives, doggies, horsies, captives, "kids," victims and other receptive parties.

How Do You Know You're A Top?

Many tops remember having toppy fantasies for as long as they can remember anything. It's not uncommon for a top to remember talking neighborhood kids into playing cops-and-robbers with lots of bondage, or teacher-and-student with lots of spanking. On the other hand, some people have their first top fantasies at puberty and some during young adulthood. Some excellent tops don't remember ever having had a top fantasy until a partner talked them into trying a light scene - and a whole new world opened up to them.

These fantasies may have caused the top lots of pain and worry. One top of our acquaintance recalls having his first bondage fantasy in the late '60s, shortly after the Tate/LaBianca murders - and spending anxious months worrying that he was turning into a mass murderer.

Catherine remembers:

I can remember having top fantasies since very early childhood, but I was well into my 20s before I recognized that these diverting thoughts – which were obsessing me to the point of making it difficult for me to function in the real world – were actually sexual in nature. And once I figured that out, it took me even longer to grasp that these marvelous, dirty, nonconsensual stories didn't have to stay fantasies, that there were people out there who would be interested in acting them out consensually with me.

So the easiest way to know if you're a top is to take a hard look at your fantasies. Being a dominant person in real life doesn't necessarily mean you're a top - many people who are hard-driving type As prefer to bottom. Nor does being a bit quiet and withdrawn in real life mean that you'll turn into Attila the Hun in scene.

On the other hand, if the idea of giving direction, taking control, inflicting strong sensation sends you into a panic, that doesn't necessarily mean you're *not* a top. Even the most experienced tops suffer from what performers call "flop sweat."

The question is: while you're jittering at the very thought of topping, is your dick getting hard or your pussy getting wet?

If you've occasionally dreamed of somehow rendering your partner completely helpless so that you can wreak your wicked will on him/her... if you find yourself looking speculatively at the belt rack in the department store, and you're not thinking about holding your pants up.... or if the thought of someone kneeling naked at your feet as s/he serves you a nice cup of tea sounds like it might be, well, your cup of tea... guess what. You may already be a top.

Does there always have to be a top and a bottom? Well, no. Some people like to play scenes in which both (or all) players are receiving sensation. ("Nipple tug-of-war," in which two people both put on nipple clamps with chains running from one person to the other and lean backwards so that both sets of tits get a nice steady pull, is a good example.) Some like scenes that involve power struggles, where nobody knows until someone "wins" who the top will be. Still others like to switch in mid-scene.

It isn't always easy to tell who's the top and who's the bottom even in one-sided scenes. For example, if Catherine orders Dossie to tie her up in a specific position and give her an exact number of cane strokes to the lower half of her butt... who's the top? Who's the bottom?

Nonetheless, it does seem to be true that the vast majority of S/M play involves at least one discernible top and one discernible bottom. Outside a given scene, these two individuals may identify as the opposite role (many tops are excellent bottoms, and many bottoms are excellent tops).

The important thing to remember in thinking about this is that whether you're an experienced top or a novice, a bottom who'd like to switch or a bottom who'd never dream of switching, or a novice with a head full of tangled fantasies and some uncertainty about which string to pull to unravel them... there's something for you in this book. So read on!

Chapter 2. What *Is* It About Topping, Anyway?

In the so-called "real world," most of us constantly struggle with power, working to empower ourselves, and to protect ourselves from being overpowered by others. This is serious business.

But power can be sexy as well as serious. In S/M, we imitate the outward appearance of those grim real-world struggles for power, while building in the safeguards we need to keep us from being genuinely harmed. We believe that one purpose of S/M is to give us a way to enjoy the "upside" of power - its sexiness and drama - without bringing along its "downside." We've heard people say, "S/M is power games for fun instead of profit," and we agree.

Building your hearth. But isn't this desire for power potentially destructive? Good question. We live in a culture of powermongers. We see all around us the ways in which power is misused to abuse those who have no power to protect themselves. So how can we, as tops, justify wanting to get our rocks off feeling like the most powerful person of all?

The popular stereotype of an S/M top is of an amoral, irresponsible and destructive person. In contrast, we find that playing with power is like playing with fire: yes, there is the possibility of destruction if we are not careful... and there is also enormous potential for constructive heat that warms and heals.

One way we make it safe to play with fire is to build an adequate fireplace, a container, a hearth. We call it "scene space," and we'll tell you about building it later. Another way we make it safe is to become wise in the ways of power (in S/M, we have lots of opportunity!). An ethical top understands power and wields it constructively, responsibly and safely.

Is all power the same? From feminist theory we have learned to distinguish between power-over and power-with. Power-over is a behavior pattern in which a person measures personal power by his or her ability to control others - you increase your own power by stealing power from somebody else. You can see this dynamic anywhere you see rigid hierarchies or chains of command, like the military.

In our experience, if your goal is to build yourself a sense of empowerment and solid self-esteem, stealing power doesn't work very well. People who strive to empower themselves this way often behave like addicts, constantly scheming to replenish a supply of power that never was truly theirs.

On the other hand, there is power-with. Power-with enables us to get more power by sharing our power with others. The more I have, the more you have. By supporting one another in our power, we get more for ourselves. Great, huh?

In any S/M exchange there is a *sharing* of power - the bottom lends his/her power to the top for the duration, the top adds power, and together they make a *lot* of voltage. The top gets to wield all this power, a form of extreme empowerment that is exciting, hot, erotic, and, as we said before, very, very sexy.

So the first big payoff for topping is that we get to ride a whole lot of power, and to be, within the agreements and boundaries of a scene, enormously powerful.

Playing in the Shadows

There is another very important reward we get from topping: the opportunity to become whole. Does that sound a little grandiose?

In S/M we get to live out roles and emotions that may be forbidden or troublemaking or unsafe in the rest of our lives. If we acted out the role of Empress of Everybody in the so-called "real world." Everybody would get angry with us and tell us to shut up. In S/M, if we want to exercise our internal bullies, eager bottoms will sit at our feet or leap to do our bidding - at least they will if we learn how to make it rewarding for them.

Tops get to act out emotions like anger, bossiness and cruelty that would be destructive in regular life. In the "hearth" of the S/M scene, there is a place for these feelings, so we get to reclaim *all* of ourselves - not just the "good" parts. We learn that our bottoms can love our most forbidden selves... and, at the same time, we learn that we have the power to explore those selves without *becoming* them, to become evil and nasty for a while yet return to our normal nice everyday selves whenever we want to.

Carl Jung believed that between the conscious and the unconscious mind lay a partially conscious area he called the "shadow." The shadow contains all those things that we have chosen to exclude from our awareness: feelings we would rather not have, desires we believe are immoral, ways in which we are more like our bullying parent than we really care to know, those stamps we stole from the office. The shadow contains all the parts of ourselves that we ourselves have rejected.

When we find a way to have those parts in the world, to eroticize them, to put them on and take them off again like suits of clothes, to receive validation - indeed, desire and love - for our most forbidden parts, we get to be more conscious, more self-accepting, and further along the road to being whole.

So What's In It For You?

We asked a number of tops what rewards they found in topping - thanks to all of them for the following list. Remember, when you read a list of other people's turn-ons, some will work for you and others will not. Don't worry - hardly anybody could like everything on this list; there are certainly a few that we ourselves have not experienced.

- *Empathy.* Near the top of most people's lists is the "contact high," the turn-on we feel in empathy with the

11

bottom's response to the physical, emotional and sexual intensity of the scene. One top describes this feeling as getting to surf the bottom's sensations.

It is certainly a truism of S/M that the bottom is on the receiving end of most of the stimulation. If empathy didn't work so well we wonder if anybody would get turned on to topping in the first place, or if we would all decide that topping is all work and no fun. But the happy truth is that you can indeed get intensely stimulated ourselves from what your partner is feeling. Both of us are amazed, after a few hours of highly technical topping, when we get to the part of the scene where the focus is on our orgasm, to experience an explosive orgasm (or several of them) - as if it had been building bigger and bigger inside us, just waiting for us to have the time to have it.

Empathy in S/M presents a wonderful paradox: as tops in role, we are often called upon to present ourselves as cold, cruel and unfeeling, when in fact we are getting our rocks off on an empathy so profound that it can approach the telepathic. So we believe that, contrary to the opinions of the uninformed, consensual sadism, dominance and topping are primarily empathic activities.

- **Creativity.** Another frequently cited delight of topping is the opportunity for creativity. We get to be the playwright, the producer, the director and the lead actor all at once. We are presented with a lump of malleable clay - the bottom - with which we can create the sculpture of our fantasies. We get to enjoy our inventiveness, our resourcefulness, our competence and our flashes of genius. We get to exercise our intuition as we figure out what will get to this particular bottom, or how to get them where we want them. We get to have our fantasy our way, to play dolls with real people: for a while we get to make the world look just the way we want it to. We play God.

- **Bigness.** When we top we get to feel *big*. It may not be okay to act huge in ordinary social interactions, and you're

usually not allowed to overwhelm people without their permission. When we top we put on a role that is about being important and powerful, a role which brings with it a lot of social respect within the S/M community. And when our bottoms respond to us in our role as giants, when they offer us their trust, their adulation, and their belief in us as we see ourselves in our fantasies – when we see ourselves enormous in our bottoms' eyes, what a blazing hot mirror!

- *Nurturing.* Catherine remembers some of her childhood fantasies in which she was doing really terrible things to very small people, so she could cradle them like dolls afterwards. Nurturing is a big part of much of S/M, and the combination of kindness and cruelty is one of the fastest ways to take a bottom down the deepest.

  How does nurturing reward the top? Well, the nurturer, again, is big, and in S/M gets to be even bigger as we practice a kind of hyper-nurturance, enveloping our bottoms, almost as if we could engulf them. As nurturing tops we may play out the roles of Good Mommy or Good Daddy, maybe in a way we didn't get to experience in our childhood, so we get a chance to rewrite history. In scene space we can elicit and reenact trauma and also be the good parent who heals the wounds. Many of the most profound psychological scenes include intense nurturance. And in a world in which nurturing energy can be in short supply, it can be a delight to create an environment in which we get to taste a whole lot of it.

- *Bullying.* In S/M we get to act out from parts of ourselves that could not be described as nice: the bully, the villain, the inquisitor, the brute, the betrayer. Wicked, wicked, wicked. And popular. Check out mainstream movies, or fiction from best-sellers to classical mythology, for verification that everybody adores a really good villain. Those bad guys are *big.* Big enough to carry all the world's ills, and create all the pain and trouble a hungry bottom could want to suffer.

And what could be more forbidden than our own nastiness? Most of us learned things from our families and our culture, or perhaps from our more primitive and essential natures, that aren't very civilized. Many people view almost all functions as interactions between victims and oppressors, so in topping we manifest our oppressor so the bottom can be in victim role, and both of us can have a powerful and erotic experience. S/M provides a safe way to be in the world for our internalized oppressor, the precious bully within.

- *Control and competence.* Another powerful reward we get from topping is the opportunity to be in control. We can be control queens with permission - even encouragement. Many tops who used to be primarily bottoms report a strong motivation in the chance to *do it right*: if you've ever been on the bottom thinking about how that knot is too loose, and if you ran another rope from just *here* to over *there* then the tension on that thigh would be released and the legs would be held perfectly open, you'll understand some of the joys of control.

  S/M is a technical sport, and a lot of us eroticize the chance to be competent, to generate perfectly balanced rope bondage, or an exquisitely timed sensory deprivation scene, or to choreograph a profound psychological journey. And when we do that well, we get to ride the scene and our bottoms, with our universe, for the moment, in complete control. How gratifying.

- *Self-knowledge.* A familiar story - "helpless captive," "shopping in the slave market," "punishing the naughty boy," those good old stories that snuggle us to sleep at night - can be the tip of the iceberg of profound psychological archetypes that we don't see clearly, like a dream or a vision. Playing these roles out in S/M can be the way in which we clarify our vision, and developing an S/M persona can become the process by which we learn more about who

15

we are. Then our bottom's response becomes the mirror in which we see ourselves more clearly, and as we choreograph the bottom's experience and stretch both of our limits in scene, we constantly create new mirrors in which we can see yet more. The possibilities are indeed endless.

What About Bottoms?

If some of the above tickles your fancy, chances are you would enjoy topping. So what about bottoms? What do they get out of this? Why would a person want to be beaten, humiliated, ordered around and otherwise inconvenienced so that you can feel big? Well, because bottoming is very, very sexy too. There is tremendous luxury in giving up responsibility and power to a top, in being small, possibly childlike, in getting nurtured while being subjected to all kinds of intense stimulations.

Fear can be arousing... the subjective experience of bondage can be so sensual as to approach a trance state... the controlled experience of pain in a safe and consensual scene can be tremendously rewarding. S/M enables us to use the body's ability to produce naturally occurring morphine-like neuro-transmitters called "endorphins" in response to painful stimuli. In "The Bottoming Book" we described in detail how pain can be processed through the body to create an endorphin high, and how ecstatic experiences of intensity and openness transmute strong physical and emotional sensation into an altered state of consciousness that we experience as extreme pleasure.

Bottoms get to see themselves in a "mirror" created by their tops. In the suggestible state of bottom space, a bottom can see himself or herself as beautiful, irresistible, big and strong or small and sweet, a precious possession or an inanimate object - with the help of the top who holds, keeps and projects that powerful imagery.

Other rewards of bottoming include getting lots of attention, as well as acting out fantasies of helplessness and other forbidden emotions (needy, pathetic, dependent, guilt-ridden) that, like their toppish counterparts, would cause lots of trouble in the real world.

How Are Tops and Bottoms Interrelated?

So tops and bottoms are interdependent - we need each other to play out our fantasy roles as well as to perform the physical acts that make us so happy. Bottoms need tops to push them off cliffs so they can fly, and tops need bottoms so they can ride the same winds, and so both can have their dreams come true. This is obvious... but the fantasies that we play with in S/M are not necessarily obvious.

The nature of the dance of S/M tends to polarize our roles to a greater extent than might be possible or healthy in the rest of our lives. Play pushes both top and bottom out to the far ends of the spectrum. Each player, in traveling further out, supports the other in going yet further. Thus as a wonderful scene progresses, the bottoms get smaller, the tops get bigger, and the larger the territory we encompass: we move to the outer ends of the spectrum, generating something like centrifugal force, spinning further and further out while holding each other safe and tight.

Whose Fantasy?

We want to mention here that not all scenes are based on fantasies, and especially not on fantasies that have detailed scripts. While many of the scenes we describe in this book are role-played scenes with narratives, that's mostly because we've chosen them to illustrate specific points - not all that many of our scenes, or those of other players we know, are based on stories. Instead, the scenes are often based on an image, an emotion, or a specific activity like bondage or flogging or anal sex.

One question that comes up when we actually sit down to negotiate a scene is whose fantasy are we playing, the top's or the bottom's? The answer is either, or both, or whatever the two of you together decide will work the best. Some bottoms are not comfortable talking about their fantasies for fear of seeming too directive, but we believe that it is a requirement for skilled and supportive bottoms to be able to tell you about their desires - as a top, you need some information to figure out what will make this scene work.

Good tops learn to support bottoms through the embarrassment of revealing their fantasies - and isn't embarrassment one of those hot forbidden emotions we love to play with? *Force* that little thing to tell you what s/he wants!

Similarly, tops need to learn to speak comfortably about their fantasies and desires. As we'll see when we talk about negotiation, tops don't just walk up to bottoms and do whatever comes to mind. Scenes are negotiated, and constructed to satisfy both bodies and imaginations while remaining within the limits of both tops and bottoms. And to find out if your fantasy is within your bottom's limits, you have to discuss it at least enough to establish those limits (everybody enjoys a surprise, but it's not kosher to tattoo "Kilroy Was Here!" on your friend's ass without permission).

Some tops feel they lose authority as a top when they agree to play all or part of a bottom's fantasy, and are offended by the idea that they may be "servicing" the bottom. We think it's inappropriate to get your ego invested in your bottom's having no desire but to please you, or no ideas of his or her own. We would be equally critical of a bottom who didn't want to hear about the top's desires and needs, or was not interested in trying out his or her fantasy.

New players often start out with one fantasy they have desired and elaborated on for years, while more seasoned tops and bottoms may enjoy many roles in many scenarios. So when we play out a bottom's fantasy we have little to lose and lots to gain. When we stretch to realize someone else's story, we enlarge our repertoire, learn new skills, and perhaps discover more ways to get turned on. Sounds like a win-win situation to us.

So we see no need to compete over whose game we are playing - we'd rather play your wonderful ideas tonight and mine tomorrow, regardless of who's in charge. Once again, we see S/M as a collaborative endeavor, in which we play with power that is shared, for the pleasure and benefit of all parties in the game.

Symbolism and Structure

As Sir Stephen remarked in "The Story of O," we are indeed fond of rituals. S/M is often characterized by a certain formality or ritual quality that reminds us of opera gowns, dress uniforms, nuns' habits and other formal signifiers.

That's because S/M is to a very real degree about symbolism - the "kidnapping" we do for erotic pleasure symbolizes the real-life kidnapping which is an arousing fantasy (since in our fantasy, the kidnappers do exactly what we want) but would be a life-shattering reality. The symbol enables us to confront our simultaneous fear of, and attraction to, the genuine horrors of the world. But we need form and structure to clarify the distinction between the symbol and the thing itself.

In S/M, form and structure enable us to take vague and abstract ideas, emotions, roles and dynamics and manifest them - pull them upwards into reality, where we can explore them and get turned on by them. Forms of play tell us a lot about what the limits are, and where the boundaries are between scene space and the rest of our lives.

Wise players study the forms of those who have gone before us, just as art students study the Old Masters (interesting choice of name, don't you think?). By building on the foundations that others have developed, we can build taller and stronger fire-places for our flames so they can leap higher, hotter and safer.

Form as represented by costume tells us what role we're playing - both from the archetypes expressed (cop, pirate, doctor) and by the function of the garments (the daddy's belt, the vampire's fangs, the goddess's sky-high heels). These symbols are also a reminder that the top has made a commitment to remain aware, contained, in control of both partners - that s/he has agreed not to fall down on the floor and thrash in ecstasy until it is safe and consonant to do so. The bottom may not dress at all, indicating vulnerability and availability, or may have his or her essential nakedness accentuated by symbols like collars or corsets, or by clothes which can be removed by the top as part of a spiritual and physical stripping away of defenses.

Bondage, even symbolic bondage such as a loop of thread holding thumbs together, is a form which limits the bottom's behavior and defines roles. So are the names which we call one another - "sir" and "boy," "mistress" and "slave," "milady" and "sirrah," "Spot" and "woof woof!"

Sometimes, our environment is our form. We enter the dungeon and become our "other selves," then leave it and become our day-to-day selves again. Our time agreements may be our form: we'll play until 3:00, then go get something to eat. Or our play itself may be our form - we agree to play until one or the other or both of us has had an orgasm, or has reached some mutually agreed upon level of stimulation.

All these forms are there to help you get as big as you can, and your bottom as small as s/he can, while ensuring your safe return to your normal size when you need to go back. Like Alice's looking glass, they enable you to wander safely through the topsy-turvy dreamscapes of fantasy, where pain is pleasure and cruelty is love.

Chapter 3. What Do Tops Do?

Finding Your Top Persona

As a top, you might be a sadistically vicious interrogator, or a sweetly sorrowful parent who's only doing this for someone's own good. You could be a mad monk out of a Ken Russell film or an eight-year-old girl blackmailing her babysitter or the evil caliph keeping his harem in order. You could be Captain Bligh, Captain Picard, Captain Hook, Captain America or even Captain Kangaroo, because the ways to be a top are limited only by your imagination.

Most of our S/M fantasies come from very deep places inside us - Catherine blushes to admit that she still has toppy fantasies about the villains on the old campy "Batman" TV show that aired in her impressionable adolescence. We draw our fantasies from the powerful archetypes found in popular culture, like movies and TV shows; from the real-world power games that simultaneously attract and horrify us (Michael Fay's judicial caning in Singapore had the whole world's shocked and titillated attention); from well-thumbed reminiscences of our own childhoods - in short, from almost any place our monkey curiosity carries us.

These fantasies are seldom sophisticated, ambiguous or even very pretty. They almost never contain negotiation or safewords (these are "safety nets" that get built into our real-world play to help make our fantasies safer to bring into reality). For these reasons, and because we're usually told that wanting to hurt, control or humiliate people is not OK, we may feel very ashamed or embarrassed about our fantasies. But once we overcome that embarrassment, what a hot and happy place our fantasy world can be to play in!

During one of our recent play dates, we originally had no particular scenario in mind. But during the one-hour drive between our houses, Catherine was idly fantasizing about being the matron in a Victorian workhouse full of girl orphans. With no small embarrassment, she shared that fantasy with Dossie over lunch. Dossie happened to be wearing a sundress that made her look about fourteen, and the roles and scenario fell easily into place from there: Dossie became the new little orphan recently brought into the workhouse, and "Miss Catherine, ma'am" spent a happy couple of hours showing her "how things is done around 'ere," and what could happen to her if she misbehaved.

Advertising people refer to radio as "theater of the mind," because a few well-chosen words and sound effects are all it takes to create an entire scenario inside the head of the listener. We think S/M is theater of the mind, too. It's a rare treat when you can set up an S/M scene with full props and costumes and dialogue; more often, a couple of items - a dashing hat, say, or a flogger that looks like something Basil Rathbone might have used on Errol Flynn - is all it takes to create and maintain an illusion. And, as the top, you get to be playwright, set designer, costume designer, director and audience.

Do you always have to have a role? A lot of our best S/M scenes have been done without recourse to any particular role - we're not Harriet Marwood or Ming the Merciless, we're simply us.

Still, though, any given scene has a "flavor" that can often be described by describing a role. A harsh scene in which limits get pushed, in which the top acts as though s/he really doesn't care what happens to the bottom, may have the flavor of a torture, rape or interrogation scene. A very nurturing scene, in which the top is giving the bottom a lot of "there, there, you can take just a *little* more" messages, may have more of a nice-mommy or nice-daddy flavor.

22

A lot of people are bashful about overt role-playing, and others simply aren't turned on by it - it seems false to them. But, just as a role-playing scene where the bottom wants to be a horsie and the top wants to be Superman is likely to run into problems, a scene where one partner wants to humiliate and the other wants to be nurtured is probably not going to work too well. So even if you're not into playing your roles overtly, it's important to be clear about what flavor of scene you want. And when we talk in this book about a "daddy scene" or an "interrogation scene," we may be talking about a scene with overt roles, props and dialogue, or we may be describing the overall flavor of the scene.

Where Are the Boundaries?

As you can see, many of the roles in this book reflect real-world power relationships of various intensities. Because we are eroticized to power, we may begin to feel that we want our play to be more and more "real" - to creep closer to the edge where the realities of consent and power begin to blur.

S/M folk sometimes describe people who play in that blurry area as "edge players." But we think *all* S/M folk are edge players.

We're all playing in a topsy-turvy world where pain equals pleasure, where fear equals arousal, where "no! no!" equals "YES!!!" Each of us may be, in our own way, trying to define the boundary where our bottoms' enjoyment of "not wanting something" turns into *really* not wanting it, and trying to expand that boundary outward bit by bit. The player whose play seems so light that you wouldn't even define it as S/M is an edge player, because s/he is in his/her own way doing something that's difficult or scary or painful, in an attempt to turn the unacceptable into the erotic: playing at his or her edge.

Catherine once did a scene with a novice bottom:

He'd never played at all before, and so I set his first scene up to be very lightweight: I tied him to the bed, blindfolded him, and simply gave him mild, sensuous sensations with different textures – fur, leather, my fingernails and so on – all over his body. If you'd asked me beforehand, I'd have told you such a scene would not be much of a turn-on for me; I was doing it as a favor to him. But as I caressed him, he began to release some deep emotions: he giggled, he writhed, he sobbed... he was just one great big live nerve ending. And I found that I was getting very turned on, because while the sensations I was giving him weren't much, they were eliciting such powerful and primal responses from him. He was getting stroked with a scrap of fur, but it was edge play for him – and that made it edge play for me too.

We deplore what Dossie has dubbed "the hierarchy of hip about heaviness." In this form of craziness, a player whose forays into branding/bullwhips/whatever have been only moderately successful is deemed superior to one whose light spankings or erotic bondage sessions have left his or her partner glowing like a 200-watt bulb. To us, the only criterion for good S/M is: did everyone involved get what they wanted from it? If the answer to that question is "yes," the session gets an automatic A-plus - whether it was a handspanking or a needle suspension.

We know one player whose mantra is "This is not a contest. This is not a contest" - repeated to himself every time he begins to try to exceed another player's accomplishments. We think this is a good mantra for us all.

When you itch to go further. Nonetheless, many of us find that the more we play, the closer we want to come to the gray area between "enough" and "too much," between consent and nonconsent. These desires may grow so strong that we feel that we're craving genuinely nonconsensual play - that we really *do* want to kidnap a stranger or whip a slave or punish a child.

We will assume that you who are reading this book are not genuinely likely to do any such thing. (If you feel that you are in danger of actually harming someone, please seek help from a therapist or counselor right away.) But when you're feeling frustrated by partners who want to stop before you're ready to, or who don't want to play the way you want to, it's easy to let the fantasies grow so strong that they begin to seem like realities. The good news is that, with patience, skill, mutual knowledge and trust, and sometimes a bit of compromise, there are usually ways to indulge those desires without harming, alienating or losing your partner.

We suggest that you spend a little time thinking objectively, if you can, about the fantasies that are driving your desire to push limits. In your fantasy, what is the turn-on? How can you tell, for example, that the bottom has been driven past limits? Is s/he begging, crying, screaming? Is there physical evidence - blood, urine, tears?

When you have a pretty clear picture of what that turn-on looks like to you, you get to the embarrassing part: describing it to your partner. You may find, to your surprise, that your bottom has been having similar fantasies, and needs only your permission to go into the headspace you've both been craving. (Begging for mercy, for example, is difficult for many bottoms, who may be worried that they will beg so effectively that you'll actually stop. Knowing that you're willing to keep going unless you hear a safeword can feel very freeing.) Or your bottom may be willing to play-act the fantasy in the way that turns you on - s/he may find that the role starts to seem very real and very arousing once s/he gives it a try.

We sometimes meet tops (and bottoms) who want to do scenes without safewords, reasoning that it is impossible to "really" push limits when the bottom can stop the scene anytime s/he wants to. A safeword is simply a code we use to communicate the status of consent. Responsible tops play consensually - the safeword is your safety net, to let you know that's what you're doing.

In our experience, the most common problem is the opposite one: bottoms who earnestly hang in there way beyond their limits and safeword too late rather than too soon. But remember - bottoms are there with you because they want to explore their limits, and they, not you, are the best judges of where those limits are. The safest and most growthful way to expand limits is with time, trust and practice: as partners play together and learn more about each other's communications style and physical limitations, they tend to use encoded safewords less and less often. But even partners who have been together for years need safewords to signal the rare but critical situations where one partner or the other has a genuine physical or emotional emergency such as illness, injury, unexpected rage, age regression and the like.

If You're Doing It, It's "Real"

Both of us cringe, hand have been known to get a bit snappish, when we hear phrases that start with "real" or "true" - "real submissive," "true Master" and so on. When you hear someone use one of those phrases, we suggest you mentally translate them into what they really mean - "someone who plays in a way I approve of."

Often, people who dismiss others as not being "real" are expressing scorn for limits which are both real and realistic, and which exist (acknowledged or unacknowledged) in all safe play. When you set yourself up an unattainable ideal S/M role, and subtract points from your estimation of your friends and yourself whenever anyone falls short of that ideal, we think you are setting yourself up for a lot of disappointment.

The player who does a light session twice a year is doing something extremely "real" - s/he is giving away or taking as much power as feels safe, healthy and sexy to him or her. So is the most extreme 24-hour-a-day, seven-day-a-week master or mistress and slave couple.

S/M is about contradiction, about paradox. A bottom who is (or pretends to be) without desires, fantasies or power is an unsafe and unhealthy bottom. A top who is (or pretends to be) without vulnerability, compromise or connection is an unsafe and unhealthy top.

If you can't understand these paradoxes - the ways in which symbolic powerlessness can empower and symbolic cruelty can sensitize - please sit down and think them through carefully. We hope that when you're through thinking, you'll realize how destructive concepts like "real dominant" and "true slave" can be, and discover the far greater joys that lie in play in which everybody's needs and wants are acknowledged, honored and met.

4. Rights and Responsibilities

"It is always wrong to wield power if you are not prepared to accept the consequences for your actions and do the work it takes to use your strength and authority with precision and fairness. A good leader is many people's servant. If being trained to become a perfect servant sounds too humiliating, you are not strong enough to withstand the temptations of wielding power."[1]

Lighting up dark places - your own and your bottom's - is a tremendous responsibility and a tremendous turn-on. While you may top *playfully*, you should never do so *frivolously*; your partner's physical and emotional well-being, and your own, are on the line. This chapter is about the kinds of responsibility you are agreeing to take on when you decide to top, and about the kinds of rewards you have a right to expect in return.

The Top's Bill of Rights

We the players of the S/M community, in order to form more perfect scenes, establish arousal, ensure domestic titillation, provide for mutual support, promote the general welfare, and secure the blessings of sadomasochism to ourselves and our play partners, do ordain and establish this Bill of Rights for dominants, sadists and all those who put their self-image and reputation on the line to get themselves and their partners off.

You have the right to clear communication. Before, during and after your play, you are entitled to receive as much

---

1. Pat Califia, *"Modern Primitives, Latex Shamans, and Ritual S/M."* From *Public Sex: The Culture of Radical Sex,* Cleis Press, 1994.

information about your partner's needs, wants and limits as s/he is capable of giving you. S/he doesn't get to withhold information for fear of scaring you off, to exaggerate his or her abilities, or to pretend not to have limits (we *all* have limits). On the other hand, s/he can't share information s/he doesn't have; a novice may not know much about his or her limits, but can still probably tell you quite a bit about his or her fantasies. Asking you to top without as much information as you can get is like asking a contractor to build a house without seeing the blueprint.

You have the right to expect support from your partner - whether you're in scene space or out of it. As we sit here writing this chapter, we're looking in our crystal ball, and it tells us that you're going to make mistakes. (We wish the lottery were this easy to predict.)

When those inevitable mistakes happen, you have the right to expect that your partner will work with you to help correct the situation promptly and efficiently, so that the two of you can go on playing - or, if things have gone too far awry to finish that particular scene, to go on being friends and to play again another time. Unless your fuck-up is malicious or unforgivably careless, you have the right to mutual non-blaming - to the assumption that you were doing your best and simply made an error.

And you have a right to your partner's friendship and support at those times when you don't feel like being a top: sometimes we all need simply to be held, sympathized with, taken out to lunch, or maybe even to get some pain or bondage for ourselves - and a bottom who withdraws from you the minute you take off your fetish gear or put down your whip isn't supporting those very human and essential needs.

You have a right to be nurtured. People's needs for nurturance vary widely, but most of us need to feel taken care of at least sometimes - even, perhaps especially, tops. We remember a scene we did together:

In this scene, Dossie was a prom queen, all in taffeta and rhinestones, and Catherine was the street hood who

kidnaps her from the prom at knifepoint to torture and rape her. It was a *very* hot scene – and it brought out some cruel and hateful aspects of Catherine that she'd never experienced before. After duly binding, stripping, beating, torturing and fucking Dossie, Catherine held her and brought her nicely back down to earth. Then we went upstairs for something to eat. In the food room, Catherine, who was by this point trembling and a bit weepy, sat at Dossie's feet and said plaintively, "Could you just pet me for a while, please?" Dossie stroked Catherine's hair and rubbed her neck and shoulders until Catherine felt quite sure that Dossie wasn't still seeing her as the nasty hoodlum, and still accepted and liked her after experiencing such a dark and shadowy self.

The moral is that accessing your shadow, as a top or as a bottom, can put you into a state of tremendous emotional vulnerability, and you may need lots of nurturing and acceptance while you are in that state. If you're not getting the kind of nurturing you want, you should ask for it - needing to be taken care of does not make you less of a top, it makes you more of a human being.

You have the right to get your needs met. A footrub? A sinkful of clean dishes? An earful of shrieks? An orgasm? Whatever it is that you need to feel like topping has been worthwhile for you, you're entitled to get that (the reverse, of course, is also true - your bottom has the right to expect to get his or her needs met as well).

But you can't expect your bottom to read your mind. If you like to hear begging, for example, say so - your bottom may have previously played with a top who insisted on stoical silence, and only be doing what s/he thinks is right. Some tops may have come of age in a milieu where genital sex is an expected part of S/M, and be dismayed and annoyed by a bottom who doesn't automatically work to get his or her top off - others could be outraged by a bottom who tries to get inside their leathers without express direction. You have to ask if you expect to get.

It sounds obvious to say that a top should tell his or her bottom how to meet his or her needs - after all, isn't that what a top does? But we've found it isn't necessarily that simple: asking for what you really want, particularly if it isn't part of a standard S/M scenario, can feel vulnerable and embarrassing. All we can tell you about that is that the payoff is, or should be, worth the vulnerability: that a scene where you and your bottom both get your needs met is almost certain to be more satisfying for both of you, and to lead to more and hotter scenes later.

You have a right to responsiveness. Very few tops enjoy pouring their energy and toppiness into a bottom who's so stoical that they can't tell whether or not s/he's enjoying it. When we top, we enjoy a bottom who gives us lots of hot sexy screaming, moaning, trembling and/or writhing, preferably with a wet pussy or hard dick for reinforcement. Other tops like watching a bottom struggle to maintain composure under stress (although a bottom who maintained composure *too* perfectly probably wouldn't be very much fun to play with). Again, ask for what you want.

You also have a right to verbal response during the scene if you want it. When we ask "How are you doing?" or "Is this working for you?," we all like to hear answers in the affirmative. However, *always* getting an affirmative answer, or getting an affirmative answer in the face of evidence to the contrary (wrap marks on a belly, for example), leaves us clueless, foundering and frustrated. If having a bottom chirp "Pardon me, sir or ma'am, but could you hit a little lower, please?" seems disrespectful to you, tell him or her to ask permission to speak first - and, upon receiving it, to give you the information you need.

Catherine sometimes tells her bottoms, "If at any time during the scene something doesn't seem right to you, and you're not *absolutely sure* that I already know it, assume that I don't and tell me about it. By the way, that's an order."

You have a right to constructive feedback. At some point within a day or two after your scene, you and your bottom will probably want to do some talking about how it went - what worked and didn't work for you and for him or her, what you might like to do differently next time, and an overview of how the scene was for both of you. During this "debriefing" - which we think is essential to both your relationship with your partner and your growth as a top - you have a right to helpful, constructive criticism. Your bottom should tell you about anything that didn't go well in such a way that you know how you can do it more successfully next time, and s/he should also tell you about the stuff that *did* go well, giving you lots of nice ego strokes along the way. Similarly, any feedback you have for your bottom also needs to be supportive and constructive. A bottom who blames you for your mistakes, tears down your performance without offering constructive suggestions, or shuts down and simply won't tell you what his or her experience was like, is not a bottom we suggest you play with twice.

The Top's List of Responsibilities

Like all rights, top's rights carry a burden of responsibility. Here are some of the responsibilities we think you take on when you agree to top:

You are responsible for knowing and stating your needs, wants and limits. When you're pretending to be Attila the Hun, Scourge of the Dungeon, it can be easy to forget that tops have limits too. But doing scenes that make you feel incompetent or disgusted or brutal is a good way to lose track of the fact that we're supposed to be having fun here, and to burn yourself out.

Everybody has needs, wants and limits. If you're new at this, you may discover some of yours by tripping over them - by doing a scene and discovering that you feel just awful, either because of something you did that you shouldn't have, or because of something you didn't do that you should have. But even if you're an old hand, your limits may change over time: Catherine spent years with a strong limit around breaking skin during play, but then discovered play piercing and has started sticking needles into people every chance she gets.

You are responsible for following through on your promises. When your play date is coming up, you may hear a chorus of "yahbut" voices in your head - "Yah, but I'm not feeling toppy." "Yah, but I didn't get a good night's sleep last night." "Yah, but I've got a lot to do afterwards and I don't want to tire myself out." "Yah, but what if I fuck up?" While we understand that pre-scene nervousness (which is often the part of you that's literally "scared of your own shadow") can be daunting, bottoms are driven insane by tops who promise playdates and don't follow through; this sort of approach/avoidance behavior is unfair and irresponsible.

If you're feeling like you want to cancel or no-show on a playdate, please don't, unless your reasons are excellent. Go, and use some of the suggestions you'll read in Chapter 9 to help yourself get turned on and into top space. We predict that you won't regret it.

You are responsible for your own and your partner's physical safety. Your bottom may or may not be able to tell you if something you're doing is causing physical harm. S/he may be so high on endorphins that s/he simply can't tell what's happening, or s/he may have gotten non-verbal and forgotten how to communicate, or s/he may simply not know what's happening. If you're not sure whether or not your bottom is able to communicate, you'll have to take the responsibility for initiating the communication. Questions like "How are your hands feeling?" or "Some of these strokes seem to be causing some bruises; is that OK?" or "Are you getting dizzy?" are perfectly all right, and if your bottom doesn't want to answer them, you should probably order him or her to.

Catherine did a scene once where her top did a good job of taking care of her physical safety:

**We were at a costume party where I was wearing a dress
made out of imitation chain mail with nothing underneath –
so I'd been sitting on a rough surface all night. I got naked,
and my friend started spanking me with his hand, then with
a hairbrush. I was having a swell time and could happily
have gone on all night... but suddenly he stopped, said, "I
think you're losing some hide here," and ended the scene
(against my vociferous protests). But sure enough, when I
got home that evening, there was a large raw blister on one
cheek of my ass, that took several weeks of cleaning and
bandaging to heal properly. If my friend had kept on going
as I demanded, the combination of the rough chain mail and
the heavy spanking might have done serious damage to my
skin – and I'd never have known it until it was too late.**

Sobriety is also important. While different players'
standards vary - some folks feel OK about very light use of
intoxicants in scene, while others do not - it is certain that if
you are too stoned or drunk to drive a car or go to work, you
should not be doing S/M. We urge extreme conservatism in the
use of intoxicants during any kind of sex, and most especially
during S/M: there is probably nothing you do that demands
better judgment and emotional balance, and using chemicals to
impair those qualities strikes us as a very bad idea. (Besides,
why on earth would you want to blur such a wonderful
experience?)

Safer sex is a subset of physical safety. Part of safeguarding
your bottom's, and your own, physical well-being is making
sure that neither of you takes anything away from the session
that you don't want - an unplanned pregnancy or a nuisance
infection or a deadly disease. Opinions change monthly as to
how risky various sexual and S/M activities are in terms of
disease transmission; we urge conservatism - when in doubt, use
a latex barrier. Don't assume that your partner's definition of
safer sex is the same as yours: discuss beforehand which
activities each of you thinks are risk-free enough to do without
a barrier, which are risky enough to require a barrier, and

which are too risky to do at all. If one of you has more conservative standards than the other, that person sets the standards, regardless of who's topping and who's bottoming - it is entirely unacceptable to subject someone to a physical risk to which they haven't consented.

Take care of your own safety, too: don't play with strangers in private, and the first few times you play with a new partner, tell a trusted friend where you are and who you're with (and make sure your play partner knows that you've taken that precaution).

You are responsible for emergency preparedness. Not everything that can go wrong in an S/M scene has anything to do with S/M. As part of taking care of your bottom's (and your own) physical safety, you should have the equipment, training and ability to handle real-world emergencies ranging from quakes and fires through heart attacks and seizures.

If you don't know what you'd do if the lights went out, if your bottom suddenly became seriously ill, or if you inadvertently started a fire in the playroom, you shouldn't do the scene until you've figured these things out. We have some suggestions later in this book, in Chapter 10.

You are responsible for caring for your equipment. If you own your own whips, sex toys, bondage equipment and so on, you are responsible for seeing that these items are carefully selected, well maintained and properly cleaned. Aside from the aesthetics of the situation (dirty or uncared-for toys are a sign of a sloppy top), poor quality or poorly maintained toys are downright dangerous - we know one top who broke a finger trying to grab a whirling handle on a badly designed winch, and we've heard many stories of bottoms pulling inadequately attached eye-bolts out of the wall and sustaining nasty falls.

While the jury is still out regarding whether or not HIV can be transmitted via uncleaned sex toys, it is certain that various other nasties, including hepatitis, can be. When you're not sure if a toy has been exposed to body fluids, assume that it's contaminated and clean it carefully. Chapter 11, and several of the books in the Resource Guide, give more detailed toy cleaning information.

You are responsible for your own and your partner's emotional safety. This may seem a little counterintuitive - after all, in the real world, we believe that people should be responsible for taking care of their own emotions and for asking for the kinds of emotional support they need. But we believe that the implied contracts of S/M are a little different, and that the usual boundaries get shifted a bit when we play together.

If Dossie were to show up for our co-authoring appointment tomorrow, and Catherine were to say to her "Dossie, I feel angry because of something you said last week," we would handle that in certain ways: Catherine would accept responsibility for her own anger and would process it herself - with Dossie's help if Dossie cared to give that help, or without it if Dossie didn't.

But when we agree to play together, there is an assumption that those adult boundaries are going to be altered - perhaps even to some degree dropped. (This is what Catherine means when she says that "S/M is ritualized codependency.") Unlike the real world, where we assume that adults are responsible for processing their own emotions and taking care of their own needs, an S/M player - particularly a bottom - may become quite dependent. Part of our responsibility as tops is caring for that bottom when s/he is in that childlike, dependent state. (If you think about it, this dictum is actually similar to our responsibility to care for a bottom's physical well-being when s/he may be too endorphined out or too deeply in bottom space to do so.)

So we believe that whether or not a bottom has asked to have their emotional safety taken care of, our responsibilities are to provide that support. As a "default," we think that a top should take the lead in discussing what kinds of stimuli are likely to trigger emotional trauma for a bottom (Was s/he abused as a child? Is s/he a victim of violent crime? Is s/he grieving a lost friend or relationship?), and in ending or altering a scene that seems to be pushing emotional buttons in an unexpected way. If a top and bottom agree to venture into difficult emotional territory, we also think the top thereby takes responsibility to be available to the bottom during any emotional "aftershocks" that ensue. (By the way, tops have aftershocks too, so we think this agreement should be mutual.)

Even if you're doing a scene that isn't particularly emotional, we think tops should expect to provide plenty of support, praise and affection - before, during and particularly after the scene. (If your bottom doesn't like this kind of nurturance, s/he should tell you so.) Taking good care of your bottom helps both of you to process the scene and to be enhanced by it, so you can go on to do more and better scenes together in the future.

5. How Do You Learn To Do This Stuff?

Okay, so you're interested. You have fantasies, you've thought about it, maybe you even have somebody who wants to play with you. So now what? Do you just rear up and snarl "On your knees, bitch" (or "boy," as the case may be)?

How do you learn to do all this complex, sexy, arcane, and potentially dangerous stuff? How to tie someone up, preferably without cutting off their circulation... how to give someone a flogging without breaking any bones... how to give commands in an obey-me-now tone of voice... how to use an enormous range of implements to inflict all kinds of different and unimaginable sensations, *and* be deft enough not to drop any of them on your own toes, *and* still feel like a top?...

For the novice top, there is a lot to learn. Start by giving yourself permission to be ignorant: it is not a crime to not know something. And even though your (and your bottom's) fantasy top may be omniscient, *you* are going to have to get down and learn. The more you can learn, and the more you are willing to learn, the better a top you will be. We feel sure you can have fun while you are learning to do all these wonderful things - we sure do.

If you live near a city that has an S/M support group, join it. Support groups regularly put on demonstrations by experienced players of various S/M skills, like flogging or play piercings, where they talk about safety information and show you how. At such groups, you can also meet and ask questions of experienced players, or perhaps join forces with another learner to share experience and support each other in the trials and tribulations of growing as a top. You may find a mentor. You may find an experienced bottom who wants to play with you and is willing to show you a few things.

Please don't let your top attitude get in the way of learning from your bottom. The bottom knows these sensations from the inside, and knows more than anyone what works and what doesn't. Also, tastes and limits vary from bottom to bottom, so even when you become experienced you're still going to need to find out what works and doesn't work for each bottom you play with.

If you have friends who are seasoned players, you can try out activities you would like to do to someone else by getting someone to do them to you. A friend of ours learned massage by getting a lot of massages and remembering what she liked: you can learn topping by bottoming, and paying attention to what works, and asking the top questions afterwards if you were too distracted (or happy) to pay attention to the technical details.

What, you say, me bottom? But I'm a top! (Dossie once had that last sentence printed on a T-shirt as a present for a top of hers.) Some people hold that it is not possible to become a good top without bottoming, without direct personal experience of the sensations you like to inflict on others. We do know good tops who never bottom, but we find them to be the exception rather than the rule. Most good players, both top and bottom, have some history of switching, and many identify as switches.

We've told you already that this book is not an instruction manual, and we have listed several good books to read in the Bibliography that will tell you how to perform various S/M activities safely and well. Be careful when reading books, especially pornography - many books are written by people with little or no experience, for fantasy purposes only, and you can't learn how to do the real part from them.

People all over the world join in conversations on the Internet or on computer bulletin boards, where you can pick up a lot of information and ask questions - but please remember to check things out because you have no way of knowing whether your source has real experience or is just dreaming. Here in San Francisco there are publicly advertised classes on S/M techniques from basic through very advanced; a few other cities have similar institutions. The San Francisco Sex Information telephone hotline is staffed with volunteers who give out information on all aspects of sexuality, including S/M. More sources of information are listed in the Resource Guide.

Do it yourself. Another resource for learning about new sensations is yourself. Try things out on yourself and see how they feel. Put a clothespin on the web between your thumb and your forefinger to find out how intense the sensation is, or put it on your chest, or your nipple, or.... If the sensation seems too intense, see if you can eroticize it by masturbating. Does this change how it feels? Are you still reading this book?

Oops! We got carried away. Here we were telling you about trying things out at home. What we *meant* to say is that we want you to practice hitting a pillow with your new whip till you can hit the same spot with all the tails together every time, experiment with bondage ideas to find out if a particular sash, belt or rope will cut off circulation or abrade the skin if you yank on it... in short, do your homework.

Start any new endeavor by thinking about what you are doing. With a new whip, for instance, think about what parts of the body have enough padding to strike safely - the ass, thighs, shoulder muscles and other well-padded parts with no exposed underlying organs can be struck with most kinds of whips, whereas backs of knees, faces and necks shouldn't be struck under most circumstances... get the idea? Some places might be okay to strike lightly but not hard. And each person has different sensitivities on different parts of their body. How will you find that out?

A basic rule of starting out doing anything new: you can't go wrong by starting out very lightly and working on up. Dossie remembers:

> When I was a real neophyte, at one of the first occasions where I saw experienced people play, I was watching two leathermen, dressed head to toe in black leather with nickel

studs gleaming everywhere, aviator sunglasses – I was completely intimidated. They were the most menacing-looking human beings I had ever been in the same room with. The top had a riding crop, and the bottom bent over a table, and I expected mayhem. What actually happened was that the top took the crop and went tap tap tap as lightly as rain over that bottom's ass. He made the skin flush with the lightest touches, bringing the blood to the skin, very patiently. I watched the bottom slowly become engaged in the sensation, swaying slightly, breathing deeper, getting turned on, all while the crop's touch was very sensual, very light. Very gradually, the top began to hit a little harder. As soon as the bottom began to jerk a little at the blows, he held steady and began to set up a rhythm for a while, not increasing the intensity, just staying right where it was beginning to hurt. I watched the bottom become entranced. Again and again, the top increased the intensity by just one notch, and the bottom became more and more responsive, both of them obviously in perfect communication with each other, almost as if they were dancing. Eventually, the top was striking with all the force he could muster, and the bottom was thrashing and yelling with wild abandon – they stayed there for a while too, savoring the experience as long as possible before it was time to come back down.

It's tough to go wrong by starting light, and some of the best floggings and canings start out as sensual scenes. Some may stay sensual, enjoying the dominance and control and the sensation without a need for intense pain. But however far you are going to go with it, starting any sensation at the lightest possible level allows the bottom to work his or her way into it as it allows you to get accustomed to the implement, work into a rhythm and get your aim adjusted so that if and when the scene escalates to a more intense level you will have, essentially, practiced.

Helpful hint number two: take your time. A fantasy top may dash in and tie up his or her victim in three seconds, but that's fantasy. What is actually very sexy is to put someone in restraints very slowly, in a ritual pace, so you can savor the entire process, and have enough time to get the knots right without fumbling. Take your time approaching your bottom's body - just because s/he is all tied up doesn't mean you should leap on his or her genitals with little glad cries and no foreplay. Spend some time touching skin; it will bring you into synch with your bottom and take him or her further down into bottom space. And when you do get to the erogenous zones, take a lot of time. Enjoy yourself. After all, your bottom can't stop you, right?

Another helpful hint: get comfortable. If you are going to spend time doing something exquisite to another person's body, you don't want to have to stop because your back hurts, so be aware of the position you are in when you start up and make sure it's going to be comfortable for a while. Some tops wear weight belts to protect their backs when they play, others recommend shoulder-stretching exercises before doing a flogging.

And don't forget to make the room comfortable. You might be wearing more clothes than your bottom, and you might also be moving around more, so remember that naked people who can't move get cold, and turn the heat up. Floggers create a wind chill factor, so turn the heat up even further - you don't want your bottom distracted by the wrong kinds of discomfort. Check to make sure lights are not in your or your bottom's eyes (unless you're doing an interrogation scene), and make sure candles are safely placed where you aren't going to knock them over. Have towels, rubber gloves, condoms, lube and whatever toys you may be using laid out where you can reach them without losing contact.

A final helpful hint: when it starts getting good, when you start getting response, when your bottom starts breathing hard or maybe writhing a little, that means you are doing something very right and you should keep on doing it. Many people make the mistake of speeding up at this point, or hitting harder, or otherwise upping the intensity, which can immediately take the bottom beyond the place where s/he was having such a good time. You'll develop a feel for when it's time to turn the volume up another notch - and stay with *that* another while - and this is how you can get to spend a very long time having lots of fun while you work your way to Nirvana.

And if you only get partway to heaven this time, please remember that there is always the future. You can choose to worry about what didn't happen in a scene, and if you wish, you can feel like a failure if the scene you play today doesn't get as far as you wanted it to. But those two leather men we described above had almost certainly played before and not gotten anywhere near that far. So value the pleasure you had today, and have confidence that you have also gained knowledge and expertise that will take you further down the road the next time you play.

As you can see, there is a lot to learn, but be reassured that most of the details will become second nature to you very quickly. The examples listed above are not a complete list, but a few ideas to get you started. And once you get started, we hope you will have a very good time learning new and wonderful ways to play for the rest of your life.

6. S/M Ethics

In the S/M scene, we give ourselves and each other permission and encouragement to explore the further reaches of our psyches and to adventure bravely down the path of the forbidden. We open ourselves up to the unknown on the dark side. And when we are open, we are terribly vulnerable.

So, in order to be open, and to be safe and healthy while we play at violation and betrayal, we believe that all players should enter into scene space with the highest of ethics, and a firm commitment to respect and honor the courage and the vulnerability that we all, tops and bottoms, bring with us into a scene. We see an S/M scene as a special and sacred space, and believe it critical that we not violate the trust or integrity of each individual in it.

Consent

Full consent in S/M, or in any other manifestation of sexuality, requires an active collaboration for the pleasure and well-being of all persons involved. We come into S/M with the intention of actively supporting each other in exploring sensation, danger and vulnerability.

Consent to any S/M scene is very specific: we consent, tops and bottoms both, to every detail, and we can choose not to consent to any item on a scene agenda.

Honesty in consent is mandatory for both tops and bottoms. You can easily understand what can happen if an eager-to-please bottom consents to some violent assault that s/he really doesn't want, and you go ahead and s/he hates it. Your safety and competence as a top are violated, and you are faced with a freaked-out or angry bottom through no fault of your own. As a top, if you consent to play a scene that you really don't feel good about, and you don't share your reservations, and you don't somehow magically get into it after you begin, then you can wind up playing an awkward and "cold" scene, with little or no connection to your bottom, who can wind up feeling abandoned, abused and violated.

Consent is only meaningful if it can be withdrawn without risking undue criticism, judgment or rejection. If a bottom or top tries something in a scene and it is genuinely unpleasant to them, they have an absolute right to interrupt a scene, renegotiate the agenda, and to have their concerns heard without blame. Respect for consent is mandatory.

Safewords. A safeword is a word agreed upon by the players in a scene that means stop, there's a problem, we need to change something, something isn't working, someone's in trouble. We establish a code word because many of us become incoherent when we are very excited - we recommend safewords that are short and easy to pronounce when breathing hard. We use code because many scenes are based on a fantasy of non-consent, and yelling "nononononono" may be part of the script.

Tops safeword too. Dossie tells the story of a time when she safeworded out of a major scene:

> My lover had wanted me to brand her for a long time, and we had planned, collected information, researched everybody else's experience and our own personal symbolism, and set up to do a ritual branding. We lived in the country, and had invited friends to come down to support this event, so there were witnesses. I had been practicing branding and felt somewhat insecure about my facility with the procedure, but spent the morning up in the ring of redwood trees over a very hot hibachi gamely branding slices of potato and turkey parts until I felt I could touch her with hot metal and not burn all the way through her. During this time, the houseguests were keeping her

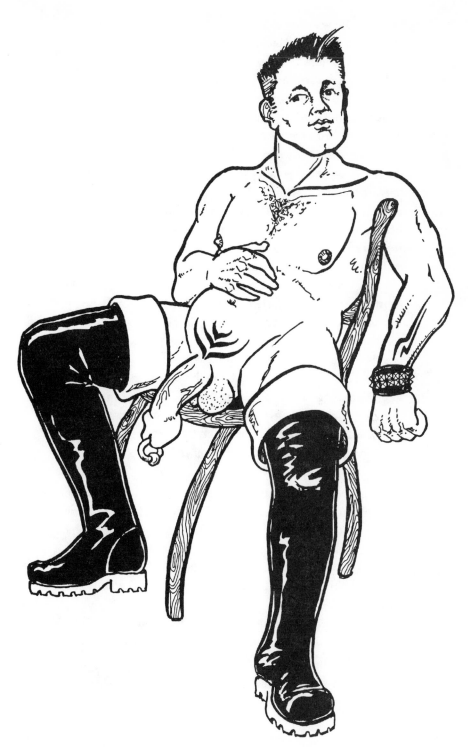

47

amused, and when we started up she was already entranced. Our ritual included a flogging to bring up the endorphins before the actual branding, but when I started to flog her it became apparent that something was wrong. Nothing I did seemed to be right for her, a very gentle stroke was too hard, she was not comfortable and neither was I. She wanted to go ahead anyway, but I decided that I could not brand her when I couldn't make connection, and that there was no way that I was going to put a serious and permanent mark on her body when things were feeling unpleasant. So I safeworded, big bad brander that I am. I felt like an idiot. Here we had brought all these people together and I had chickened out. *And* my lover wasn't happy about it, and it took awhile to bring her back down onto the planet from her tranced-out space – it was dire. I must have apologized forty or fifty times to our guests, who were very supportive and reassuring, bless their hearts. I reminded myself over and over, as I remind you now: it is possible, actually not very difficult, to have an experience of extreme public embarrassment, live through it, and be fine afterwards. Which we were. I now think the first time was a rehearsal, and perhaps we both needed to know that we could back out. About a month later, we got together with two friends and pulled the branding off without a hitch, and with much delight.

Whenever a player safewords, this is an occasion for mutual support. We understand that nobody safewords from a happy place, and that all of our egos feel frail and kind of runty when we need to back out of a scene. It is completely unethical to respond with scorn or ridicule to a person who has safeworded: S/M is not about a competition, we are not playing against each other.

As tops, we have noticed that if we are having a good time and our bottom safewords, our initial feelings may not be happy. Whaddaya mean you don't like that? I do all this work and you don't appreciate it? I'm hot for being in control and you want me to stop? We have felt real anger and felt challenged in our top role... and, on a deeper level, we have felt put down, hurt and rejected. It is okay to have these feelings. It is not okay to act on them. Take three deep breaths and everybody start taking care of each other.

Sometimes bottoms get so deeply engaged in a scene that they fail to safeword, or forget, or so profoundly believe in the fantasy that it doesn't occur to them. Dossie remembers a scene in which a top offered her a choice of something or other: "I felt very confused. Some distant part of me vaguely remembered having made choices, but the response from my state of consciousness at that time was, Choose? I am not a thing that chooses." So then what is the top's responsibility?

If a bottom does not safeword and you don't pick up on what's going on, and this *will* happen if you play long enough and well enough, there is no blame. However, it is still your responsibility to monitor for physical safety as best you can. As ethical tops we make a commitment to never knowingly harm our bottoms. To this end we check in regularly to make sure that things are going the way we think they are, and we constantly monitor the physical and emotional safety of our bottoms. If a bottom is beyond safewording, and you as the top feel unsure about how far you should go, it is your responsibility to slow down or stop the scene and get into communication with the bottom to make sure you have informed consent. If you have to bring the bottom back into reality to do this, please remember that you helped get them into that altered state in the first place, so presumably you can help get them back there again as soon as you are sure of what's going on.

Respecting Limits

Respect and honor your bottom's limits. Respect and honor your own limits. Respect means nobody gets put down or belittled, top or bottom, for whatever limits they may have. Looking for loopholes in a bottom's stated limits is cheating, as is concealing your own agenda with half-truths or omissions.

"Well, you didn't *say* I *couldn't* shave your head" is not a substitute for consent. Ethical players negotiate scenes in good faith.

Confidentiality. In recent years, due to the energetic work of members of our community, S/M has become less stigmatized, and some of us may not feel as great a need to keep our sex lives in the closet as others. This is wonderful progress, and we look forward to the day when none of us needs to walk through the world fearing oppression if our secrets were known. However, that time is not yet here, and many of us could be at tremendous risk if the wrong people - our landlords, employers, students, parents, children - were to find out about our interest in S/M.

So we still need to keep information about others that we acquire at support groups and play parties confidential. Do not assume that just because you are totally uncloseted, everyone else should be. Do not assume that because a player is well-known in the community that that person has no closets - we know players who use assumed names because outing might jeopardize important parts of their lives like joint custody of their children. Do not assume that you know what another person's requirements for discretion are, or that another person lives their lives as openly as you do - just protect everybody's privacy.

Are there exceptions to confidentiality? Yes. We can look to the legal and ethical standards of medical and therapeutic confidentiality for guidelines: it is acceptable, and at times even required, to violate confidentiality when there is significant danger of harm to any person. If a person assaults you, you don't keep it a secret, you call the police. Gossip may sometimes have an unpleasant but necessary function within the community to warn others of players who in your experience are in some way dangerous. (It is not ethical, however, to badmouth players simply because you don't like them or are angry with them.) We try to balance negative gossip with goodmouthing: making a point of introducing people to each other with full regard for their prowess, and letting others in the community know when a player does something wonderful.

Boundaries and Blaming

Any problem in ethics, including the complex dilemmas we may run into when we pretend to be unethical, can be clarified by looking at it from the point of view of boundaries. *Personal* boundaries are found wherever we understand that I end and you begin. Within the boundary of scene space, our personal boundaries will probably be very different than they are in the outside world... so when I know which boundaries are in effect right now, I know when it's the right time to violate you.

People also have *internal* boundaries that tell us what state of consciousness we are in. For those of us who play a number of roles - top, bottom, Doctor Mean, Dracula, little boy, baby girl - we open and change our internal boundaries to get in and out of role, often unconsciously. The more conscious we can be about this, the safer we will be, and the more adept at getting into (and back out of) the role we want to play right now.

Internal boundaries tell us the difference between a thought, a wish, a fantasy and a dream. For the S/M player, the boundary between fantasy and reality is all-important: it is how we maintain our sanity, and how we maintain our identities as big bad mean ethical loving sadists.

Blaming, a special case of bad boundaries, consists of refusing to own and take the responsibility for our own stuff, our feelings, dilemmas, and actions. Of course, occasions in which a problem is truly one person's fault do happen, and need to be respected... but we believe most problems that crop up between people actually belong to both or all of them. When we blame, we fail to shoulder our part of the burden; we project the responsibilty for whatever is wrong onto another, usually to protect ourselves from feeling terribly guilty or anxious. When we blame, we also disempower ourselves - if it's all *your* fault, then *I* must be impotent.

So we recommend that you approach conflict that arises from play (or any other relationships, for that matter) in a nonjudgmental mode. In our culture, you can observe many people attempting to resolve a problem by discovering whose fault it is (the comic author Fran Lebowitz says "It isn't whether you win or lose, it's where you lay the blame"), as if most of our dilemmas were caused by somebody doing something wrong. In S/M, we can make tops wrong by accusing them of anger, attitude or abuse when a scene doesn't work out well. We make bottoms wrong by accusing them of being needy, resistant or smart-ass.

Blaming may alleviate our anxiety on a short-term basis, but in the long run resolves nothing. If, on the other hand, you can put your judgments aside and operate on your own feelings while you listen to your partner's feelings, you may be able to come to an understanding that keeps you in sympathy with each other *and* empowers you to take care of the problem so you can continue playing and having a good time.

Hearing feedback. Good post-scene etiquette is for the top to call the bottom within a few days of a scene to check in and make sure everything's okay, and bottoms will respect you and feel well cared for when you do. Mostly you will hear flattering feedback that can be a big help if you're having top drop. This is also an occasion to ask the bottom if there was anything in that scene that they would change, or do differently in the future. So you can generate the occasion for your bottom to tell you about that little bruise in the wrong place, or something that was sharp or harsh or otherwise not optimal for them. Our experience is that bottoms often tell us what we could have done harder or longer or louder or stronger. Greed is a wonderful thing in a pig slut bottom.

Sometimes you will hear from a bottom who is unhappy or distressed about part of the scene, or some of the things you did. When this happens, it is important, and difficult, that you not get lost in your ego. That ego may be screaming "But you writhed and squealed, I was sure you liked it, I felt like God Almighty, whaddaya mean you didn't like it!" And you need to put your ego aside and listen.

If your bottom is a good communicator, with any luck s/he will offer negative feedback without a lot of blaming, in a supportive and nonjudgmental manner. But everybody is not well-versed in communication skills, and when something goes wrong in a scene bottoms are often genuinely frightened or even a little freaked - so you may wind up with complaints coming at you like arrows, from a person who is seriously upset with you.

We do play with scary imagery, and it sometimes happens that a bottom is so frightened by a scene that s/he feels unable to communicate directly with the top - so you may find out through a third party, or, worse yet, a public accusation. Most of us have a hard time not getting defensive when someone is angry with us, and we may be justified in that we can blame the bottom for blaming us, or for failing to talk to us directly, or for gossiping. And even when you are right, defensiveness and counterattack will still only make the problem worse.

We feel the best thing for you to do in this situation is to listen to the bottom who is upset with you, and hear him or her out thoroughly whether you agree or not. Be aware that this is happening because the bottom feels bad - hurt or scared or whatever. By being willing to listen to that person's feelings, you validate them - and that might solve the problem right there.

If you feel you did something wrong, the best thing to do is own it. Remember that apologizing won't make you less of a top. And if you don't feel you were wrong, you can still say you're sorry that someone feels bad, or that something you did left them feeling bad. Apologizing won't make you wrong either: you *are* sorry that they feel bad.

Most often these conflicts arise from misunderstandings rather than malice. When you listen, and when you express your regrets about a play partner's unpleasant experience, then that person may become willing to listen to you, and the two of you are in a good position to clear up misunderstandings, and stay friends.

Respecting Persons

Tops and bottoms both have identities beyond the roles they play in S/M. We understand that tops and bottoms are both complete human beings of equal stature and importance, deserving of respect. Their needs are equally important, their wisdom is to be regarded, their opinions worth hearing. When bottoms play at being degraded, do they truly become less than their tops? We think not.

S/M works best when bottoms honor and value the gift the tops bring to them, with respect for the hard work and personal vulnerability that is involved. S/M works best when tops honor and value the gift the bottom brings: the bottom power that fuels the trust and belief which transform us into tops.

7. On Your Mark... Get Set...

Communication Skills for Tops

To get ready to do a scene, you first need to share some information with your bottom, negotiating the specific details of what you are and are not going to do. Ideally when you're done, you will know what your bottom's limits are and your bottom will know what your limits are. You will have also exchanged some information about what turns each of you on and some ideas about what you both might like to try - knowledge gleaned from fantasies or scenes you have played in the past. You should each have a clear idea of each other's needs - those parts of play that are so essential to you that without them the scene would not be worth doing. Everybody's needs are valid, everybody's needs are important. Including the top's.

During a good negotiation, you will also share some wants - things that you and the bottom know that you like or would like to try. Think of the wants as the ingredients from which you will construct a fabulous dinner: how much easier it is to cook when you have lots of ingredients to choose from! Obviously, you'll want to collect all the wants you can get from both of you. But that's not always easy to do.

Getting the information you need. When a bottom tells a top what s/he likes, it can feel like ordering the top around, which doesn't fit with many players' fantasy roles. Further-more, many bottoms are embarrassed by their fantasies, and plagued with the belief that whatever it is that they want, it must be too much to ask for. A professional dominatrix of our acquaintance once got so frustrated with a client who would say only "I only want to please you, Mistress," that she told him facetiously, "Then give me the money and leave; I'll go to a movie."

So how do you get that information without getting out the rubber hose (yet)? There are many ways to support a bottom in expressing his or her desires. Just knowing that you *want* this information gives your bottom permission to share it. Sometimes it is easier to deal with this information outside scene space, so many tops instruct their bottoms to write a letter expressing their desires and stating limits. In person, but not in scene space, sharing fantasies and ideas can be fun once you both get into it; you can always start by sharing some interest of your own and then inviting your bottom to contribute.

In scene space, you can order your bottom to communicate and make it part of the play. So your bottom is embarrassed? Goody. You can tie him or her up and wait until s/he speaks - and you can wait a long time, if that's what it takes. You can offer positive feedback: "That's hot, I like that, what a good idea, mmmmmm nasty!"

Bottoms generally like it when tops say what they want: "I want your ass right now, I want to bend you over that table, I really want to see you on your knees in front of me, what a sweet sight."

Do inquire about limits, pain tolerance, safer sex, physical limits like asthma, contact lenses, muscle and joint problems that might make some positions uncomfortable. Bottoms should know enough to tell you their limits without prompting, but if you ask it makes it easier - the bottom doesn't feel so much like s/he is sitting there with a long list of "don't do this and don't do that," in danger of falling into terminal negativity.

I-messages. We have talked before about the damage done to hot play by blaming. Here we would like to introduce an alternative borrowed from the couples-counseling literature: the I-message. Communications experts noticed that we often speak in you-messages, like "You are making me angry, you should be different, you always give me a hard time when I want to have fun, you never want to do what I want." The you-message almost always sounds like an accusation or an attack, and the person to whom it is addressed most commonly becomes defensive and tries to explain themselves and why they are not wrong. When they do that they have stopped listening to you.

The I-message basically means I share something of my internal reality, my feelings, my desires, my thoughts, my beliefs, like: "I feel angry, I would like something to change, I want to have fun, I want to find some things that we both want to do." The I-message is clearly about our own stuff, and once we make it clear that we can be responsible for our stuff and willing to take the risk of sharing it, our partners become free to own their own feelings and problems and desires, and to speak their own truth, from their own tender places near the heart. And we are fond of exposed tender places, aren't we?

Needy bottoms. Sometimes our roles get in the way of good communication. As tops, we have permission in scene space to be mean, nasty, intrusive and overpowering; similarly, bottoms may go into their own emotional spaces and become childish, dependent, needy and clinging. In real life we often respond to neediness by closing our boundaries and pushing people away, perhaps becoming annoyed and judgmental in the process. In S/M, while ideally we both get to open our boundaries in a sort of controlled codependence that would not be acceptable in real life, the urge to withdraw in response to neediness can still be strong.

So how do you find a more constructive way to deal with neediness in scene space? First, you get to have limits. So as a top, if you really hate a particular kind of play that makes your partner seem uncomfortably needy, you can choose not to play that kind of scene.

If you feel pressured by indirect hints, you can insist that the bottom ask directly for what s/he wants. This can actually be healing: a person who uses neediness and manipulation may have grown up in a family where there was no straightforward way to get his or her needs met (s/he learned this behavior

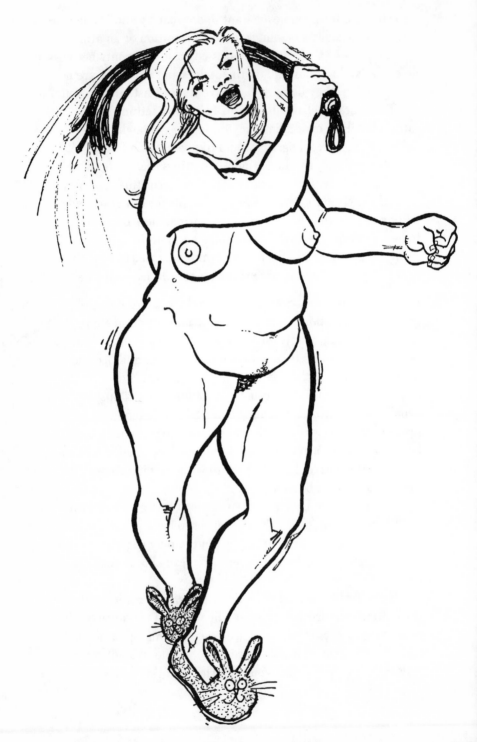

somewhere, right?), so getting positive strokes for asking for what s/he wants can be a wonderful revelation.

Or you can negotiate a scene that includes neediness or dependency by making an agreement that the bottom will bring in the adult self when asked: "I want to talk with the grown-up now." It may take a few moments for the bottom to switch states of consciousness, but the ability to switch from roles to reality is worth developing - practice makes perfect.

Black holes. "Black hole" is a terribly rude name for bottoms who do not put out enough visible response for you to feel confident that you have any idea what is going on with them. They may or may not be having a good time, but their demeanor is so impassive that you can't tell. And if you can't tell what does or does not work for this bottom, without feedback, how can you know when it is safe to proceed? Response is the top's safety information, and it is also the top's reward. This is our theater, and the bottom's response is our applause.

It's tempting to deal with unresponsive bottoms by judging - this person is a lousy bottom, and I won't play with him or her again. But what if you like this bottom? What if s/he is your friend? Your lover?

Is there anything you can do to make this bottom responsive? Remember that nobody is born knowing how to do this stuff, and anybody can learn. In "The Bottoming Book," we discussed the process of getting a scene off the ground and of finding your turn-on as a bottom, and we recommended acting "as if." If a bottom breathes hard and works his or her body, s/he will actually get more turned on, and provide feedback for you to play against. It doesn't hurt for the top to model turn-on and interest too - think of all that wonderful gay male porn where the top is always saying "Oooooh, yeah!" in throaty tones. You can breathe hard and grind your groin against your bottom, for example, to get you both turned on and set a good example.

Back when you were negotiating what you were going to do in this scene, perhaps you remembered to ask some questions about how this bottom gets turned on. Suck on the neck? Blow in the ear? Spit in the face? It's always reassuring when you know what to do.

You can tell a bottom, even without leaving role, that you need more response, that you can't tell if the scene is working or not. Dossie remembers:

> **The first time I topped at a party I was flogging a woman I didn't know very well, and wasn't sure if it was okay to hit harder. I didn't want to interrupt the scene to ask, especially because there were people watching, and then I got a great idea. In my best mean voice I growled, "If you want me to hit you harder you better get that ass up there where I can get at it!" And she did, and I did, and it was great.**

So this bottom knew how to get what she wanted - and, for that matter, that she could reduce the intensity by pulling away. Thus you can instruct your bottom in exactly what kind of body language you want to hear.

S/M Activities that Require Special Consent

Disagreements and hard feelings sometimes arise between players when one player takes for granted that it is okay to do something that the other player assumes should not be done without ascertaining consent prior to the scene. This happens in the vanilla world too: a good example might be anal penetration, for which an unspoken etiquette dictates that you find out how your partner feels about his or her asshole before you plunge in and yell "Surprise!"

S/M opens up the potential for an enormous range of activity, and what is bread-and-butter ordinary for one player might be something the other person has never heard of. A difference of opinion in this area may get discovered in an atmosphere of extreme adrenaline rush, which can make it difficult to maintain emotional equilibrium. So allow a moment to come down, and please remember that these are not occasions for fault and blame, but for understanding differences in customs.

We will present here a list of things that some people might think would require specific consent - with the proviso that just about nobody would agree with every single item on our list. Still, we think that if you're not certain about consent, you have to ask.

- *Sex.* Some people take for granted that an S/M scene will include something resembling genital sex or orgasm-producing activity, and will be very disappointed if they play with someone who does not have that as a given. Even if you and your partner have agreed to be sexual, you need to agree on what kinds of sexual behaviors are OK - assplay, as we mentioned earlier, is one common limit. People also make assumptions about safer sex that are better to negotiate: for instance, there is wide difference of opinion about the relative safety of oral sex, and a lot of disagreement in some heterosexual and lesbian communities about whether safer sex is important at all. (Just in case you couldn't guess, we think it is.)

- *Marks.* Temporary marks, like bruises or welts that last a few days, are common occurrences in S/M. However, some people - such as those with vanilla partners at home - might have problems with them, so it's probably a good idea to ask about marks before you haul out the cast-iron cane. (A gynecologist once asked Dossie if she got those bruises riding a horse - Dossie responded, "No.") We strongly recommend that you never promise a new bottom you won't leave marks, because different skins react very differently to the same stimulus and you can never know for sure how *this* bottom's body will react.

  Cuttings or piercings intended to be temporary can sometimes leave marks that last a lot longer than intended, so even if someone gives you permission to open their skin it's not a good idea to carve your initials on their ass, or indulge a taste for silly graffiti. The skin should probably not be opened at all without consent, and deliberate permanent marks must always be negotiated.

- *Pain.* It's easy to assume that any bottom enjoys pain, so we will remind you that Dossie did not play with pain for her first several years in S/M: pain is an acquired taste for a lot of folk. We are both very happy that we've acquired it, but would still look askance at someone who would inflict intense pain on us without some reason to believe that we would enjoy it.

- *Phobias and turnoffs.* Many of us have one or more psychological phobias, images or associations - rape, slavery, prostitution, child abuse and Nazis are common ones - that make us so unhappy or frightened in the real world that we do not wish to play with them in S/M. Some people have serious phobias about needles, fire, electricity or blood, and may not be sophisticated enough to know that these can be S/M activities. (We do play with fear, but we do so consensually.) Few people assume an easy comfort level with shit, and piss is more accepted in some communities than others.

- *High-risk play.* Some forms of play have much higher risks of injury or death than others. Breath control and above-the-waist electricity can stop hearts, sometimes permanently. Firearms play, no matter how careful you think you're being with an "unloaded" gun, can go tragically wrong, as can playing with real-world danger like speeding cars and skyscraper balconies. Play involving drugs or alcohol impairs bottoms' perception of damage being done to their bodies, and reduces tops' judgment and inhibitions. We think all these require both partners' explicit consent, and a lot of planning for safety.

- *Limits of scene space.* Scenes that expand the agreed-upon limits of scene space require special consent - for instance, inviting other people to join a scene should be checked with your bottom, because if you get your bottom all tied up and hot and bothered and then introduce your three friends who just arrived, s/he might get a little outraged. You also include additional, nonconsensual participants if you play visibly in public, like if you chain your bottom to a parking meter and go inside for a cappucino. It is very important to have explicit consent if you want to record a scene in photos or on video or audiotape: many people have strong and valid limits about pictures of themselves in extremely embarrassing positions possibly being seen by other people.

- *Emotional limits.* Scenes likely to evoke profound emotional conflict require special consent, both from the bottom and from the top. Such scenes may involve abandonment, extreme humiliation, regression to child or baby states, and real-world emotions, especially anger. These are all "button-pushers," and can evoke much more extreme responses than you bargained for. We find it particularly important to agree that we will not take anger we have about real conflict into a scene - it is really unlikely that you can improve your relationship by physically punishing your partner for disagreeing with you, and to do so violates the boundary between scene/fantasy space and reality.

Limits for Tops

As tops, we have the same responsibility as bottoms to know our own limits. We can start by being honest about what we want and what we don't want. A good exercise to clarify this is called "Yes, No and Maybe." Make a list of all the sexual and S/M activities you can think of, and then divide them into three categories - *yes, no* and *maybe. Yes* is what you know you like, *no* is what you know you don't like, and *maybe* is all those things that might be hot if the time were right, or you were really turned on, or you could get someone who already knows how to teach you. This exercise can be fun to do with your partner or in a group - but if you feel that to be a real stud top you ought to be ready for anything, maybe you should try it alone the first time so you can be honest with yourself. On your *yes* list you will probably find plenty of things you like, and the *maybe* list promises plenty of hot stuff to explore. Respect your own *no* list as you would your bottom's.

It is particularly important to know and honor the limits of your knowledge and skill. It can be embarrassing if a bottom approaches you with a new eight-foot bullwhip and wants you and only you to crack it over his or her ass, forcing you to admit that you have no idea how to operate that thing. But remember, it would be a lot more embarrassing if you tried to do it and failed, and even worse if you wound up injuring the bottom - a very real possibility, as throwing a bullwhip is dangerous and requires a tremendous amount of training and practice.

If your fantasy of being a top requires you to be all-knowing, that's a fine fantasy, and you still have to know your limits. And good bottoms will respect your honesty - at least, if we said we'd never done something before and a bottom said "Aw, c'mon," we would wonder a lot about that bottom's respect for safety.

Making room for your own needs. Where do sex and physical stimulation for the top fit into your scene agenda? Many of us have some difficulty feeling like a big bad top when we are on our backs with our legs in the air squealing in ecstasy. Some tops like to focus on what they are doing to the bottom during the scene, and arrange for their own orgasm afterwards. Some of us top first, then switch to the bottom role to get stimulated. Some of us order our bottoms not to touch us at all during a scene because it is distracting.

You can make a space during your scene for your own stimulation, and you can negotiate that with your bottom. For instance, you might like a butt plug in your ass and a vibrator on your cock or clit while your pleasure slave pulls on the chain between your nipple clamps - so why not? Bottoms may or may not have access to a whole lot of initiative while they are in role, but most of them are good at following directions. So make a clear agreement with your bottom before the scene starts, untie your bottom and order him or her to molest you in your favorite way when the time is right, and remember that your bottom, just like you, might need to focus on what s/he is doing to you - so this might not be the best time to yank off a clamp while your tender parts are between his or her teeth. Or then again...

8. Wild Scenes We Have Known

Since no amount of abstract instruction carries the same weight as the stuff that happens in the real world, we thought we'd tell you about a few scenes that we or our friends have done.

Please don't take these scenes as blueprints, or even as ideals of "perfect" scenes. They're just representative of a few different playstyles, ways of building energy and connecting and having hot sexy fun together. (At least, they were for us!)

Scene #1: A sensation scene at a party, played by Catherine and a female friend.

B. and I are close friends, but had played together before only once, in a very limited way; this would be our first full-on scene together. We are both het-identified bi women, both experienced players, and while we're both switches, she is more comfortable in the bottom role. I knew from our discussions ahead of time that she enjoyed flagellation of all kinds, particularly on her butt, and that she was fond of play piercing and of both vaginal and anal penetration. While she is comfortable with dominant/submissive roleplay, she doesn't need it to enjoy straight sensation play; since it isn't a preference of mine, we decided to pass on any kind of mental control and simply go for the "high" of strong sensation. We agreed on safewords and were ready to go.

We arrived at the party somewhat early, so we had our choice of bondage equipment. To start out, we chose a large cable-spool table, padded with vinyl and surrounded by handles. B. told me that bondage makes her feel uncomfortably confined and that she would prefer simply to be told to hold still. She hopped onto the table and I told her to lie face down, placing a thick pad of paper towels under her pussy. I unfastened her garters and took down her stockings, but left her corset in place; her butt was my target for this part of the evening.

I started out with a heavy soft suede flogger and began gently flogging her butt and upper thighs. I could tell she was hardly feeling these strokes, but I built them up fairly slowly anyway, swinging overhand from her left side, then from her right. By the time the strokes got fairly hard, she was beginning to get turned on – she was arching her butt up to meet the suede and moaning loudly. I moved down to her feet and pulled them apart to spread her legs, then began flogging her butt from below in a figure-eight configuration, quite hard. Her response grew vivid enough that I was pretty sure she'd come if I kept it up, and I didn't want that to happen yet. So I finished with a few more strokes and switched to a harsher, stingier braided cat, using the same pattern of first from the left side, then from the right, then in a figure-eight from below. I thought that this sensation would be more painful and less sexual for her, and judging from her reaction, it was... but she was obviously still having a good time. (It was somewhere around this time that I moved up to her head to see how she was doing, and she saw that I was laughing and began to get a little uptight, thinking that I was laughing at her. I said, "No, I'm just laughing because you're so unbelievably fucking wonderful.")

I wanted her next sensation to be solider, not as spread out as the multi-tailed implements I'd been using so far. I got out a heavy leather strap and began swinging that from the side. She was obviously working pretty hard to handle that sensation; she started rolling from side to side to avoid the blows, so I used my left hand to press the small of her back down toward the table while I whipped with my right.

(I wasn't sure if being held down physically would trigger her aversion to bondage, so I watched her reactions carefully. It seemed OK, and I was enjoying it, so I kept it up.) The sensation of the strap didn't seem to be turning her on much, though, and I wanted to keep her sexual arousal high. I put a glove on my right hand and lubed a couple of fingers and began to explore her asshole. One finger went in effortlessly, and so did two. She was moaning and wriggling against my fingers – OK, great. I got a medium-sized butt plug out of my bag, stretched a condom over it, lubed it up, and inserted it. It went in with no difficulty at all, and she reacted with dramatic and visible arousal. I resumed strapping her, pausing to wiggle the plug a bit whenever the balance between pain and arousal seemed to be tipping too far.

Next I got out an experiment – a birch rod (a bundle of long whippy birch switches bound together at the handle and spreading out into a broomlike spray). She'd never felt a birch before, and I'd only used one a couple of times before, so we weren't sure how this would work out. Since she'd been reacting more positively to thuddy toys than to stingy ones, my guess was that she'd have a hard time with something as stingy as the birch. I started hitting her ass with it. She went quite still, her back arched, hands braced against the table and shoulders and head up. Obviously I'd guessed right – this was a tough sensation for her. But she rose to the challenge. I went a little harder. Her face was working with the effort to process the sensation. I was enjoying birching her a lot, but I wanted this scene to be more about pleasure/pain than straight pain, so I didn't push it too hard. I rubbed and massaged her butt a bit to diffuse the sting, and told her she'd been great.

Time for something more fun. I took out a clublike rod of heavy Teflon – a thuddy instrument that has to be used extremely carefully, since it could break bones with a missed or overly hard blow. I tried a couple of not-too-hard strokes on her lower butt and she began to moan almost immediately. I hit a bit harder and she began to writhe. Experimentally, I tapped the base of the butt plug with the club a couple of times and she began to act like she was about to come, so I grabbed the plug and began to wiggle and thrust it. She came almost immediately, loudly and enthusiastically. I alternated hitting her with the club and getting her off with the plug a couple more times until she was panting and limp.

At last, the grand finale – the canes, which I knew were her favorite and mine. I started with my lightest cane, a medium-width whippy rattan one. I gave her one trial moderate-strength stroke, and when I saw her reaction I knew we were onto something. I hit harder, mostly giving her about fifteen seconds between strokes to process the sensation, but occasionally making her work harder by giving her two or even three in quick succession. Her moans were low-pitched and the motion of her hips told me that she was finding the cane strokes erotic. But she'd taken quite a bit by now, and since I didn't really know too much about how well her body recovered from heavy beatings, I didn't want to push my luck, so I began to think about winding the session down.

I switched to a different cane – a manmade one, a bit thicker and quite a bit heavier in weight. I gave her a dozen or so blows with it, walking from one side of the table to the other between strokes so that she had plenty of time to work with the sensation. I reached for the butt plug again, manipulating it with my right hand and pressing against her pubic mound with my left, bringing her to one final giant orgasm. Then I told her she could choose a number between two and ten to receive with the heavy cane, and then we'd be done. She chose four. I gave them to her as hard as she could take, and felt the endorphins rush in her and me as she stretched to meet my challenge. And then the scene was over.

We both got caught up in a tremendous fit of the giggles, composed of equal parts, I think, of endorphins, relief and triumph (we'd *done* it!). I got up on the table with her and held her and we smooched and giggled for a while. When she felt ready to get up, I helped her off the table and swept the toys any old which way into the bag (I could always reorganize them later) and went back out into the social area looking for food and drink. We spent the next hour or so cuddling, nibbling, chatting and watching other scenes together.

The next morning, before I had a chance to call her to see how she was doing, I found an e-mail waiting for me raving about what a wonderful time she'd had and how colorful her backside was looking. It felt great to receive it.

Scene #2: A role-play scene, played by "Akasha," a novice top friend.

I woke up with great difficulty and realized my mind was full of thoughts of domination, weird fantasies about devices that I did not own but wished I did. I thought of my friend Richard, and a wonderful night we had shared many months before.

I called him and found him still in bed. I said, "God, I am really having a problem today."

He shifted in his sheets, I could hear it, and said, "Hungry?"

I was doodling, cracking pencil leads and then throwing them away. "Yes," I said, and I was sort of half shaking, just wanting to make him beg on the phone, make him get out of his warm bed and kneel down, make him whimper, do anything. But I wanted more, so I held back and asked him to see me.

He half moaned and sighed, yawned again, and told me he had class that night. I told him to meet me afterward. He paused, and I felt like I was going to die.

"Richard, please. I'm going crazy. Do this for me, OK?"

"You want to hurt me?" he said softly, making me face it. This was back when it was still hard for me to accept that I enjoyed making men suffer.

It's difficult to describe what a day like that feels like, waiting for the hours to go by, trying to concentrate on work, going one step at a time. When I am in that mindframe I can smell everything in the air, I can feel mist against my face in the cold air. The moon is more illuminated, the sound of my feet in puddles as I walk somehow thrills me with a feeling of authority.

I arrived at the cafe a few minutes early and waited in the lobby. Richard arrived a few minutes late. When I stood up and hugged him he laughed softly into my ear, "How're you doing?"

I just moaned and started fingering his hair, tugging at it a little. We parted and I looked at him again, blinking. I felt weak, numb. I wanted to take him by the hair and force him to his knees. Instead I said weakly, "You probably haven't eaten yet. Can I buy you dinner?"

When his food arrived I stole his silverware and he laughed. "I'm serious," I told him in a low voice. "I am feeding you this entire meal."

His eyes searched around the room and he lowered his voice, "Come on, people will see. We can take care of you when we get home. Let me eat."

Any other night I wouldn't think twice about him eating dinner across from me. But in that mood, on that night, I wanted to be the one feeding him. I wanted to make him part his lips each time I lifted the spoon. I wanted to make him beg with his eyes for more, or look at me longingly. Or I wanted to force him to do it.

I leaned over the table and we argued a bit about it, finally compromising in that I would feed him the first few bites and then let him finish. Knowing that he hated doing it but would submit to it for a few minutes was enough for now.

When we got into my room he sat on the edge of my bed then finally lay down, spreading his arms out and sighing tiredly. I slid down and moved on top of him, moving my hands up to his wrists and holding them down there. His eyes flickered open and he stared at me expressionlessly, waiting.

I consider it true, deep headspace when I am capable, without hesitation, of exercising acts of cruelty or power as if they were second nature. These are things that I would never do in a normal state of mind. On that night I slipped into it relatively easily, maybe because I had been lingering around the edges of it for so long.

I set up a series of short scenes, because my appetite was varied and I wanted to satisfy it all. Sometimes I want total resistance, sometimes I want fear, sometimes I want pathetic, eager submission. That night I wanted them all.

I used every single restraint device on him that I had, in every position I could imagine. I kept a hand over his mouth most of the night and wrestled him to the ground three or four different times, ordering him to feign resistance until I hurt him into submitting.

I roleplayed kidnapping him, interrogating him, seducing him, and fucking him. I had an orgasm just from the way he felt against me as I took him against his will, one hand holding his head back by a fistful of hair and the other over his mouth to muffle his protests.

For the grand finale I put him in my chair and handcuffed his wrists behind his back, taking my wall mirror down and putting it behind him so I could see his wrists and enjoy the way they looked while still facing him.

I put water in his hair to simulate sweat and messed it up, tied his ankles together, and told him I was going to kill him.

He put his head down solemnly and I walked around a bit, touching his skin gently, telling him how pretty and helpless he looked. He shifted, and struggled uselessly, then

73

lifted his head to me and looked at me with his teeth clenched, saying "You have to let me go. Don't do this to me."

I leaned down and held his face in my hands, putting my lips close to his, licking them gently. "Kiss me goodbye, my tortured slave."

He shut his eyes and leaned forward to kiss me, hungry, passionate, as if to seduce me with his mouth and tongue. Ths kiss was long, desperate, and when I broke from it he was breathing hard.

His eyes were pleading, yet strong. "I'm not afraid to die," he said softly.

He always knew the things to say. He was begging, yet he was strong. He was submitting, but he was still powerful. He amazed me.

We had played these execution scenes before so I didn't need to give him any instruction. He was to pretend he had about three minutes left to live, locked in some airtight chamber or given some poisonous gas, and he was to struggle yet remain brave until the moment I came to save him from his fate.

And he really knew how to play it. Perfectly, yet differently every time. The way he pulled at the handcuffs, letting them cut into his wrists as if it didn't matter,. The way he threw his head back to breathe with such pained difficulty, the way he looked at me through wet bangs with desperation, his lashes damp with tears.

I felt so close to orgasm, but it was a different sort of satisfaction. I just watched, emotionless, as his struggles became weaker and his breathing more labored.

Then it hit me, at once, it was like a sensual overload, like an orgasm but of the mind. I shivered, I felt a cold sweat on my body and suddenly I wanted to cry, I thought, "God, what am I doing to him?" I unfastened him quickly and slid into his arms, shaking, telling him I was sorry. He laughed softly into my ear and told me it was okay, that he was acting, and that I needn't feel bad.

But feeling bad makes me feel better, so I spent some time crying, letting him reassure me. We lay down in the bed together and eventually fell asleep after I had sufficient reassurance.

Waking up the next morning I felt a different kind of exhaustion. It's impossible to explain how much dom headspace rips the energy right out of you. Sometimes it takes me days to recover.

Scene #3: A scene at a party, played by our friend Bill and a stranger.

We don't say a word. We've never met before. We're just two horny guys at a sex party. He wanders into an empty room, giving me that "Come hither" look recognized by queer men everywhere. In the room, he is seated on the couch, legs spread, touching himself through the one-piece latex suit covering his trunk. It has short sleeves and legs.

This is a rubber fetish party, my first. I feel a bit inadequate in my standard-issue leather vest and Levi's. I lower my face to his. My intuition is working tonight. I correctly guess that he likes being nibbled on the neck – prefers it to sloppy, wet kisses. He writhes beneath me. I press one hand firmly into his pectorals, pinning him as I nip into him more intensely, lips covering teeth. His breathing deepens. My fingers massage the hot latex suit. There's a zipper down the front. I pull it down to the spot between his broad pecs, exposing a splay of scattered brown hairs. He looks up at me – large brown eyes. I kiss him dryly on the mouth. We begin dry-kissing. Our breath is hot.

I reach inside the zipper, kneading and pinching his exposed pectoral flesh. It feels like I'm invading him, molesting him. This makes my dick jump. I notice through his jumpsuit that I'm having the same effect on his. I slide my knee up to his balls and press as I pinch his nipples through the latex. I start slapping his inner thighs. They're also warm from the latex, and it feels so good.

75

I remove my vest and pull the front of my black T-shirt over my neck, exposing my chest. I place his hands over my largish nipples, and we begin tugging each other's nipples, his still covered in latex. I begin slapping them with my hands. It feels so satisfying to slap this boy through his hot, tight rubber skin. I take my dick out, fully hard now, and slap it against his thighs, which makes it even harder – it almost hurts.

I pull a small bottle of lube out of a pocket and squeeze some onto my dick. I jack it off in front of him, slapping it against my outstretched palm. I open up a rubber and squeeze some lube into it, wiping off my sticky hand and rolling the affair down my swollen shaft. I put it up to his lips, and he hungrily gobbles it down. My knee slides to his groin again, and I stroke his fine brown hair. Usually I don't much like condoms for sucking dick, but in this scene, it's become one more piece of latex to fetishize. I pull out another one and try to place it around my nuts. This provides us with some comic relief as I, then he, try to trap the stubborn balls unsuccessfully. Finally I shrug and we laugh a bit.

He looks so fucking hot in that fucking suit that I start squeezing him all over as if he's the last guy I'll ever get to touch and I'm trying to carve the experience into the deepest corner of my brain. I want to rip him out of his kinky rubber armor, and yet I want to keep him trapped inside it forever, all tantalizingly displayed and hot to the touch.

I squeeze his well-developed biceps and broad, fleshy shoulders; run my fingers through his beautiful hair; squeeze his pointy nipples and his love-handles, and finally his hot, hard dick. I begin slapping it with the backs of my fingers, gently at first, worried that I'll slap too hard and take him out of the scene. But he obviously likes it, so I slap harder and harder, squeezing his ample balls. I hold his balls and gaze intently into his eyes. His nostrils flare.

Out of nowhere come the backs of my fingers, slapping him lightly across one cheek. The eyes widen. I kiss him dryly on the mouth. Then again. Slap. Kiss. Slap. Kiss. I feel surges of blood through his clenched balls. "Take it out," I hiss. It's the first time either of us has spoken in ten minutes of anonymous sex. He scrambles to comply, sitting up and beginning to unzip. "Slowly," I say. "Turn me on."

I grab my rubberized dick and jack off, pinching my nipples, both of us now showing off for each other. He slides his fingers down his stomach slowly, pulling the zipper to its end. He gingerly pries his moist cockflesh loose from the clutching rubber sheath, then the balls. He raises his eyebrows, gesturing toward my lube. I hold up the bottle and squeeze some onto his fingers. He works it onto his expanding dick. I draw closer and slip my hands under the open suit and really work his nipples now. His dick gets enormous – this kid has a dick that I can't get both my hands to cover.

I hand him a condom. He takes it out and I squirt a bit of the lube into it. He rolls it down his sticky dick, where it barely reaches bottom. Then I kneel between his knees and take it in my mouth, biting the head between my teeth and tickling his balls. He's working my nipples just the way I like, and soon the whole hot tube is throbbing down my throat and I'm biting him on just the other side of the condom, near his nuts. I can tell he's amazed, like not too many guys can do this to him. And I'm certainly not one of those tops who thinks that cocksucking is the station of the bottom. Quite the contrary – I use my dominant, forceful attitude to get boys like this one all hot and bothered, and then show them what a champion dick-chomper I am once their dicks are really stiff.

So I milk this groaning boy for maybe three minutes with my well-trained throat muscles, and then I begin jacking him off with both hands. He wants some lube, so I give him the bottle again, and he starts jacking off my condom-clad cock with his sticky hand. I grab his dick near its base and start slapping it into my palm. I feel a new tension building in his thighs, and as I slap and jerk his dick, I mutter, "Yeah, fucker. That dick's gonna shoot. Gonna fill up this rubber with hot cream. Gonna dump your fat load into this tube. Gonna slap it around till you fuckin' come, rubberboy. Gonna ticke your fat balls till you squirt –" And then he's *doing* it, twisting and gasping, that big boner of his making that little nipple on the condom tip *very* full indeed. I tickle him under the ridge until he can't take any more. I stand, stretching my cramped legs, figuring that will be all, but he reaches out and grasps my still-hard dick, jacking me off.

Now normally, I could never get off by being jacked, much less through a condom, but I'm so turned on that in two minutes I'm bellowing and spurting my load into that rubber, amazed, my entire body trembling. We catch our breath, staring at each other and grinning like idiots.

Soon we will get up from this couch, shed our jizz-filled condoms, wash up and quickly become separated by increasing numbers of people, miles, hours, days – but right now we're just two blissed-out guys, happy to be in this room together, no longer horny.

9. Go!

All the negotiation, planning, scheming and fantasizing in the world never quite prepare you for that moment when you're standing there, face to face with the bottom of your dreams, who is breathing a little bit fast and looking at you with an expectant gleam in his or her eyes. Omigod... *now* what am I supposed to do?

We suggest that before you get to that critical moment, you spend a little (or a lot of) time thinking your scene through. Try to build a fantasy around the person you're playing with and the kind of scene you've agreed to play. (Catherine likes to do this while masturbating.) Be as far out as you like in your fantasy; you can always revise later when you bring the fantasy into reality.

That fantasy will be the core of the scene you do together. We guarantee that the scene will not go exactly the way it did in your fantasy... reality is never that willing to conform to our expectations. But if your fantasy has your gorgeous captive first kissing your boots, then getting trussed up like a Christmas turkey, then getting flogged and fucked, you have at least an outline for your scene.

Don't script too tightly. If your satisfaction in this scene depends on your bottom saying certain words, or resisting in just the right manner, you'd better make sure s/he knows it, or s/he is very likely to react the wrong way:

> As part of a public demonstration, Catherine (as the sadistic butch prison warden) was threatening Dossie (as the innocent and wrongly imprisoned "good girl") with a cavity

search. It would have been very inappropriate to actually *do* a cavity search in front of an audience of strangers, so Catherine assumed that Dossie would resist, thus giving The Warden an excuse to punish The Girl. Unfortunately, she forgot to mention this plan to Dossie, who got deeply enough into the role that it didn't occur to her to refuse – leaving Catherine standing there with a glob of lube on her gloved finger and a foolish expression on her face, frantically trying to signal subtly to Dossie that she should please for heaven's sake resist so they could get on with the scene.

Catherine made the mistake of overplanning - of making the scene dependent on the bottom's reaction, without ensuring that the bottom would react the way she needed. If you want your bottom to resist, to capitulate, to beg or to struggle, you'd better make that desire clear up front or you're likely to get stuck improvising in ways that might not work for either of you.

On the other hand, underplanning - going into a scene with no idea of what you're going to do or what sequence you're going to do it in - is a surefire recipe for what Dossie calls "blank-paperitis," that brain-dead feeling when you look at the bottom and can't begin to imagine what might be a good thing to do next.

We like to go into a scene with an "outline" of possible activities - a menu that we can move through or skip around or even ignore if we think of something better to do, but that's always there to fall back on if we feel stuck. Catherine likes to plan an outline with two or three times as many items on it as she could ever actually do in a single scene, so she has plenty of choices and can go with the flow of her own energy and the bottom's reactions.

What Do You Do First?

Well, first you panic - at least a little. This is the challenging point. But have courage. Remember, we have faith in you.

In the beginning, your job is to get both yourself and your bottom into a sexy, susceptible headspace: a space in which you are powerful and terrible, and s/he is malleable and helpless before your implacable will.

We find that it's a good idea to start a scene with some sort of ritual that defines the beginning of the scene and starts to get everybody turned on. A hug is good for scenes that have a nurturing, connected feeling. For a slave-type scene, you can have a ritual of putting on the bottom's collar: many tops like to have their bottoms kneel at their feet and kiss the collar before it is placed around the bottom's neck. Touching the bottom's shoulders, back or neck establishes connection in a relaxed and soothing way. Simply standing the bottom a few feet away and having him or her hold quite still, with eyes lowered, and then turn around slowly - while you examine every inch of his or her body, your eyes burning with lust - can be a hot beginning. Catherine sometimes likes to have the bottom leave the room and come back in, with the understanding that once s/he re-enters the room, the scene has begun. Putting on some bondage can be a good start for many scenes. In other words, just about any beginning can work, as long as it serves the dual purpose of connecting you and your partner and turning you on.

Getting _yourself_ turned on. If you're lucky, you'll already be turned on and feeling like the King or Queen of Hell before you begin - but neither of us is usually that lucky; we usually have to *do* something to get turned on and into top space.

Is there something physical that you know turns you on, makes you feel toppy? Catherine feels toppy when someone kneels in front of her and sucks her nipples. Do you like having your boots kissed? Your feet rubbed? Is there a name you like to be called? Tell your bottom how to do what you like; be specific. S/he'll start to feel submissive and under your control, and you'll start to get turned on.

Sometimes you can convince yourself that you're a top simply by acting like one. Be bossy, be forceful - it's okay if it doesn't feel "natural" at first; imitate your favorite movie villain, or a top whose style you've admired at parties. As you start to act like a top, you'll probably start to feel a little excited. And the more turned on you feel, the more natural the topping will seem, and the more turned on you'll get, and...

Your bottom will notice your arousal and your toppiness and start to get turned on, too, and will add his or her energy to the drama you're building. And before you know it, there you'll both be - nicely in role, wildly excited and having an absolutely wonderful time.

Building. Once you've established scene space with a proper beginning, you can start building some momentum. For most scenes, you want to begin slowly and build gradually. (Interrogation and terror scenes can be exceptions.) If you're playing with sensation, start with the gentlest - sensual stroking or erotic pinching, or some slow-building strokes from a nice soft thuddy flogger. If your scene is more about domination and control, you may want to start with some orders that you know the bottom will not find too intense (either too demanding or too rewarding) — some posture training, say, or an order for the bottom to lightly stimulate you to get you in the mood. Save the really difficult tasks for later when the bottom is "warmed up" and deeply into role, and the ones you know s/he really loves as a reward for doing the difficult ones.

Escalate slowly. If you've started with your softest mellowest flogger, step up to something a bit heavier. Add a bit more bondage to restrict your captive's movement a little more. Start getting a bit pickier about how your commands are carried out. Challenge your bottom by requiring him or her to do something that requires concentration as s/he accepts increasing stimulation. (Catherine once played with a top who required that she address him by obscene names, each one different, as he caned her: "One, thank you, dickhead! Two, thank you, fuckwad! Three, thank you, shit-for-brains!")

You don't have to continue to escalate; one of the arts of topping is to take the bottom right up to the edge where s/he thinks s/he can't stand it any more, then back off for a while and do something nicer, then go up to that same place and perhaps a little beyond, then back off again...

Impulse topping. Occasionally, while partway into a scene that you've planned carefully, you'll be struck by a sudden

83

inspiration. Following your instinct at such a moment can be risky, particularly if the bottom is expecting something different. But, if your inspiration isn't a limit for the bottom, it may turn out to be your intuition guiding you toward something wonderful; some of our best moments in scene have been impromptu impulses of this kind.

On the other hand, sometimes you'll come up totally dry - with a bad case of the "blank-paperitis" we mentioned earlier. A good strategy for blank-paperitis is to do whatever worked last time, or, if you're in the middle of a scene, you can backtrack to do some more of whatever was working well earlier: there's no rule against more of a good thing.

One top we know taught us another excellent strategy for this moment: do nothing. Simply stop and re-center yourself. Take a deep breath or two. Look at yourself and the bottom. Wait. Inspiration will come. (The bottom isn't going anywhere.) This can seem like a very long moment, but really, it's usually only a minute or so.

Keeping It Going

Good tops are full of all kinds of sneaky ways to keep a scene going without breaking the energy of the scene.

A lot of the ideas we'll talk about in this section break down into two segments: ways to keep the energy going in a scene that is supportive and nurturing, and ways to accomplish the same goal in a scene that's harsh and is built around a fantasy of nonconsent. In both cases, you're trying to do the same things - to get support and information for yourself and to provide support and encouragement for your bottom - but the way that you accomplish those goals will depend on what role you're playing.

Taking control. An important thing to remember is that your goal is to "turn off your bottom's brain" - to enable him or her to melt into a malleable, will-less state of arousal and hypersensuality. The more control, verbal and physical, that you exert, the easier it will be for your bottom to relinquish control to you.

It's a good idea to offer your bottom as few choices as possible. "Lie down on the bed" is not such a great order, because it leaves too many questions open in the bottom's mind. "Lie down on the bed, face down, with your head facing the headboard, your legs together and your arms outspread" is better.

You may still want to offer your bottom choices as part of a head trip - "Six with the cane or 50 with the flogger?... You choose." But do so intentionally, and make it clear that you're offering the choice not because you're floundering but because you enjoy seeing the bottom struggle with the decision.

It can work very well to take control of a bottom in a physical way as well: pushing, grabbing, dragging, holding down. We did a scene that played with this sense of physical control:

> Dossie was a recently captured slavegirl in a country where she didn't speak the language; Catherine was a new owner who wasn't the talkative type. While Dossie begged, whined, offered bribes, fumed and refused, Catherine simply physically forced her (with a little help from a few floggers and canes and paddles) to kneel, to dance, to suck Catherine's breasts, to masturbate, and other critical "slave skills." For a couple of verbalists like us, it was a fabulously freeing scene – Dossie couldn't talk her way out of it, and Catherine found herself able to be physically rough, with hairpulling, shoving, armtwisting and so on, in a way that's usually difficult for her.

Giving clear, forceful directions can be difficult for many tops (perhaps especially women, who are culturally enjoined against being directive). An exercise Catherine teaches in her workshops for novice female dominants is to have the bottoms rub their mistresses' feet as the mistresses give specific directions about where to rub, how hard and in what rhythm. Although this exercise may sound simple, it is difficult for many attendees. If you have trouble giving orders, it might be a good way for you to practice this important skill.

Asking for direction. While the fantasy of much S/M play is that the top is taking his or her pleasure without regard to what the bottom wants, the reality is that you're doing this for mutual enjoyment - and you can't attain mutual enjoyment without some guidance from your bottom about what s/he is enjoying. But most bottoms don't like to feel like they're running the scene (if they wanted to run scenes, they'd be tops!), so you need to figure out ways to get the information you need without seeming to relinquish control.

Some tops like to hold a proposed toy to their bottom's lips to be kissed before they use it, thus building delicious anticipation at the same time as they give the bottom an opportunity to voice any concerns. Others enjoy having the bottom choose which toy s/he wants to experience; we know one who likes to lay out all his toys, then tell his bottom, "Bring me one item to give you pain and one to give you pleasure."

Other ways of asking for direction are verbal - and in these, tone of voice and turn of phrase matter a lot. You know and we know that the sentences "I'd like to cane you now, would that be OK?" and "You're about to get a caning you'll never forget, you little slut" really mean pretty much the same thing, but they certainly don't feel the same to your bottom.

The trick to asking for direction from top space is to phrase the request in such a way that it sounds like you're demanding it for your own pleasure, not fumbling around trying to figure out what will please your bottom.

How to be supportive. Bottoms need a lot of support when they're doing their thing, and, depending on the flavor of scene you're doing, there are a lot of different ways you can offer it.

If a bottom is doing something intense and difficult for you, s/he deserves and needs praise. If your scene has a nurturing tone, you simply may want to offer that praise: "I'm proud of you" or "You took that really well" or "You look so beautiful doing that." On the other hand, very few interrogators compliment their victims on how well they take their torture.

So if you're role-playing a scene of nonconsent or harshness, you have to be more subtle - but a muttered comment about the stubbornness of this particular victim accomplishes the same goal without breaking role: "Ah, she has spirit, I like that! More to break."

A particularly devious top trick is to use the lowered boundaries of scene space to "implant" messages of self-esteem. We've done a couple of scenes together in which Catherine is a schoolmistressy authority figure and Dossie is a young girl; Catherine enjoys telling Dossie that "a pretty little thing like you is going to be *very* popular with the big girls around here" - creating a nice sense of dread as she builds Dossie's mental self-image.

It can also be very helpful to "coach" your bottom through the tough parts by reminding him or her to do things like breathe and relax, kind of like a labor coach. If you're being a supportive top, you can simply tell your bottom what you want him or her to do: "breathe along with me" or "relax your butt muscles" or "listen to the music." If you're being a mean top, you may have to get a little more creative. "I want to hear you scream" accomplishes the same goal as reminding your partner to breathe (it takes oxygen to scream), but sends shivers up the spine in a totally different way. You can also *order* your bottom to do something like relaxing his or her muscles (with appropriate penalties if they tense up).

How can you tell what's going on with your bottom?
One of the highest arts of topping is "reading" a bottom to tell whether they're panicky and out of control, or relaxed and enjoying themselves, or so deeply into role that they can't communicate verbally, or voraciously aroused.

The first thing to remember about reading a bottom is - *when in doubt, ask.* But each bottom has his or her own ways of displaying what's going on, and the more often you play with a particular bottom, the better you'll get at reading those signs.

Breathing is often a reliable indicator of a bottom's headspace. A bottom who is breathing fast and raggedly, high up in the chest, may be in trouble (and if you let that bottom go on breathing that way, s/he may very well get further into trouble - hyperventilation breeds panic). On the other hand, a bottom who is breathing from deep in the chest cavity, with long, even breaths, is processing quite nicely, thank you. If the bottom is making noise, high-pitched screams may indicate tension, while low moans are often produced by a bottom who's having a nice time - on the other hand, we have one friend who isn't beginning to enjoy herself until she hits E over high C, so do allow for individual differences.

Physical tension is a signpost too. A bottom whose muscles are hard as rocks and quivering with energy may be getting pushed close to, or past, limits - or may be approaching orgasm. You can help such a bottom relax by stroking or kneading the tense muscles, or even taking hold of the body part with your hand and moving it around. This will also prevent your bottom from coming until you are good and ready for him or her to do so.

Some bottoms have special habits that they exhibit when they're nearing their limits (Catherine curses). Watch for these.

Tears are kind of a special case. Some bottoms love to cry in scene, find it very cathartic and would be terribly disappointed if you stopped. Others cry only if something is seriously disturbing them; their tears mean they need you to stop the scene and take care of them. If your bottom begins to cry and hasn't told you how to handle it, ask.

Checking in. Since bottoms occasionally forget how to safeword for one reason or another, we think it's a good idea for a top to have a mechanism s/he can use to "check in" to make sure that everything's still basically OK.

Many people check in verbally. "Still with me?" or "Do you remember your safeword?" are easy and readily understandable. However, they can be inappropriate for some scenes (prison guards rarely ask their victims if they're enjoying themselves), plus bottoms can sometimes get too nonverbal to respond properly.

In his book <u>SM 101: A Realistic Introduction</u>, Jay Wiseman suggests the "two squeezes" check-in: the top takes hold of some part of the bottom's body (often the hand) and gives it two firm squeezes. The bottom lets the top know that s/he's OK by taking hold of some part of the top's body and giving it two squeezes back. If the top doesn't get the two return squeezes, s/he tries once again; if the squeezes still aren't forthcoming, s/he assumes that something's wrong and that it's time to break role and talk.

Calibrating your bottom. Many tops, when playing for the first time with a new bottom (or with a new toy on a long-time bottom), use some variant of a "one to ten" strategy. Usually, the top gives the bottom a very gentle stimulus and says, "That was a 'one' on a scale of one to ten. When you're ready for another one, say a number that tells me how intense you want it." The top spends several minutes letting the bottom "call the shots" in this way, learning about the bottom's reactions as s/he goes. Eventually, when the bottom seems to be getting a little bored, the top says, "If you're ready to stop calling numbers and let me decide force and timing on my own, let me know." The bottom can go on one-to-tenning for as long as s/he needs to feel comfortable, and the top gets a good idea of how well the bottom can handle this particular sensation.

Bottomless pits and "The Forever Place." Sometimes, a bottom will get so endorphin-y or go under so deeply that s/he feels like s/he just wants to go on doing this forever and ever and ever. A bottom who is in this condition will not be able to tell you if you are doing damage to his or her body or mind. S/he may go very still, no longer struggling or making noise - this can be scary if you're not ready for it. Or s/he may still be moaning and crying, but be unable to respond to simple questions or orders. Or s/he may seem fine - Dossie grins and giggles, appearing deceptively on top of it all.

If your bottom goes into "The Forever Place," that places an extra burden of responsibility on you; s/he has no judgment, so you have to provide enough for both of you. Keep an extra-close eye on physical signals like welts, bruises, abrasions and blisters, and watch for dizziness, faintness and nausea (all signs that the bottom is beginning to "overload" and may be on the

verge of fainting). Be ultra-respectful of the limits the two of
you agreed on beforehand: a bottom in "The Forever Place"
may be absolutely thrilled to see the brass knuckles that s/he
said "absolutely not" to, but that doesn't make it OK to use
them - such a bottom's consent is no longer very meaningful.

Bottoms who never seem to get enough are called,
somewhat ruefully, "bottomless pits." Such bottoms can be
frustrating for a top, because you can wear yourself to a
sweating panting frazzle and still get a wistful "Are we done
already?" for your trouble. Some tops like to keep one or more
very intense toys or techniques for use in convincing the
bottom who thinks s/he can never get enough.

Dossie remembers a public performance she once gave:

In the early '80s, two other women and I produced an erotic
performance, the first public S/M demonstration in San
Francisco woman-space as far as I know. We had staged a
kidnapping of a "random" victim from the audience
(actually my lover), and made a big point of establishing
consent so the audience wouldn't freak out – including
having my "victim" select the whip I would beat her with,
which was a relatively gentle braided cat. We had planned
a counting scene for a birthday beating, in which she was
supposed to control the length and intensity of the beating
by counting strokes at the number she was comfortable
with... so the scene started out "one – whack – two – whack
– three – whack – three – whack – three – whack" and so on.
Our agreement was that when we got close to her birthday
age, I would hit her as hard as she liked and end at 33. Well,
she got into the Forever Place and forgot she was supposed
to want to stop, and kept counting "30, 30, 30." I couldn't
get her attention, and I couldn't very well break the rules of
play I had so carefully established, so eventually I had to give
up, announce that she had won, congratulate her and escort
her off the stage, hoping nobody would notice me shushing
her when she wanted to know why I had stopped when it
was feeling so good.

Closure. Ending the scene is one of the most important factors in helping make sure you and your bottom will both remember the scene fondly later. A sudden, unexpected or clumsy ending can take all the joy out of a scene that's been pretty nice up until that moment.

Ending a scene takes place in three parts: preparation, closure and aftercare. During the preparation stage, while you're still actually playing, you need to signal to the bottom that the scene will end soon, so s/he can begin to come back into the real world and pull himself or herself together. Dossie likes to pick out a fairly heavy toy such as a cane, show it to the bottom, and ask the bottom to pick how many heavy strokes between one and ten (or twenty, or fifty) s/he is ready to take before ending the scene.

If your scene is more about control than sensation, you may want to give the bottom a particularly difficult task - "repeat the following phrase 100 times, without error, while acting as my footstool" - with the understanding that the scene will end when s/he completes the task to your satisfaction. You can string something like this out according to your own judgment by choosing how picky you want to get about what constitutes successful completion of the task.

The main thing to remember about closure is to avoid suddenness. Withdrawing from your bottom while s/he's still floating around out in bottom space is clumsy and unkind (and, occasionally, dangerous). Give your partner plenty of warning, in whatever way works for both of you, that the scene is drawing to an end.

Winding down. After the formal scene is over, most players want and need some decompression time - hugging, cuddling, talking, dozing, eating, showering, whatever it takes to stabilize both of you back in the real world. (We offered a fairly lengthy set of suggestions for decompression in "The Bottoming Book.") It's not a good idea to let your bottom attempt complex or dangerous tasks right after a scene, when s/he may still be endorphined out and perhaps still in suggestible bottom space.

91

An S/M scene is not over until both (or all) of you have returned to the real world, to a more or less functional mental state, intimately connected and happy as clams, albeit perhaps a little stupid. This is a good time to relax and enjoy the connection. Some traditions have it that after a scene the bottom should scurry about and clean up the toys, but we prefer to wait until the bottom is recovered enough to do so without breaking anything. We like to respect and enjoy the general incompetence of warm fuzzy endorphined-out bottoms, and share in that state ourselves.

So invest some time in snuggling, sharing something to eat or drink, perhaps a warm bath (hot tubs are great for this!). You can rub any sore muscles, or have your bottom rub yours. Putting icepacks on bruises, brushing hair, washing any body parts that might have gotten sticky - grooming behaviors feel good here, and are a nice way to indicate caring nurturance.

Sometimes, especially after a particularly intense scene when you've been a very good top, your bottom may need support in returning to normal consciousness. If your bottom spaces out and you feel like you can't quite reach him or her, stay close and in physical contact. If you stay connected, you can probably enjoy the spaced-out feeling too. Allow a little time. Call the person by name; Dossie likes to blow in their ears. Touch him or her firmly, rub muscles, and gently move joints. A glass of water or something to eat is always grounding. Ask about the journey - talking gets us back in our heads - and welcome your friend back. Remember, if your bottom goes very far out it's probably because you were a very good top.

And how about you? How do you return to normal consciousness after you've been playing God? It's a mistake to think that aftercare is offered for the bottom's sake only. Many tops need this kind of warmth and reassurance as well, to remind them that they're not really the mean nasty horrible bullies they were acting like just a few minutes before. And you probably don't want to try running a staff meeting or driving the Indy 500 right after a scene, either; tops get endorphin-y, too, and bossy top energy - which can be a problem in the real world - can't be turned off like a faucet.

So share the cool-down cycle with your bottom. Luxuriate. If there's something you like after a scene, let your bottom know, and help your bottom take care of you. If your orgasm is scheduled for after the scene, check in with your bottom to make sure s/he has recovered enough to make love to you with all the energy and focus you've been looking forward to - you'll get the best treatment if you're not in a hurry. Remember, you're playing with someone you *like* (at least we hope you are!); take the time to enjoy his or her company as you float gently back to reality.

10. And If It Doesn't Go The Way You Planned?

We believe that if you never ever ever have a scene go haywire, with unexpected physical or emotional consequences, you probably aren't taking enough risks. After all, the reason most of us do S/M is to explore territories that we find a little risky and challenging; if you're sticking so close to the center of the trail that you never get lost in the woods, you may want to reconsider your pathway.

The standard by which tops should be judged isn't in how seldom their scenes go wrong (within, of course, basic standards of safety and consent); it's in how well they handle it when things *do* go wrong. So let's talk a bit about the kinds of things that cause problems in scenes, and how you can handle them when they come up.

Emotional glitches. In our experience, by far the most common scene mishap is an unforeseen emotional reaction on the part of a participant - panic, anger, grief, regression or other intense emotion. "Freak-outs" happen for a variety of reasons: flashbacks to buried memories of abuse or trauma; one or another partner "forgetting" that the scene is supposed to be playful and consensual, and getting the role and the reality confused; real-world emotion inadvertently sneaking into scene space... the possibilities are manifold.

There is no way to reliably prevent emotional mishaps, but there are ways to minimize their frequency. Nobody knows themselves well enough to predict *all* their own reactions and hot buttons, but telling your partner about any touchy aspects of your background or belief system will help him or her to navigate cautiously. (Yes, we're off on that old honesty thing again.) It's also a very good idea to actively encourage your new bottom to share this kind of information with you, so you don't cavalierly snap your snazzy new Smith and Wesson handcuffs onto someone who was recently brutalized by an abusive cop. (This doesn't mean you should never play around someone's traumas, but it does mean you should do so only with proper negotiation, safeguards and cautions.)

Still, with all the good intentions and good negotiations in the world, freak-outs will happen. And your first challenge as a top is to figure out when they're happening, which may not always be as easy as it seems. Someone who's freaking out may be unable to use their safeword, so you can't rely on that signpost. A dramatic change in response - when someone who's been thrashing and screaming suddenly gets quiet and still, or someone who's been acting happy and turned on suddenly begins to cry or struggle - is cause for concern. So is unwillingness or inability to respond to simple questions or directions. A freak-out may be subtler than that... Catherine remembers:

> I was doing a scene with a regular but still fairly new play partner – basically a straightforward cock & ball torture scene, although we'd been discussing beforehand his fantasy about being a captive soldier getting tortured by an Indian maiden. Things were going along fine for an hour or so. I noticed at one point, though, that he had turned his head so that we were no longer making eye contact, and he didn't seem to be talking much. I asked, "Are you still with me?" and he responded in sort of an odd voice, "I'm not sure..." so I got him out of the bondage fast. Later, he explained that the fantasy had started to seem real to him – he was really beginning to believe that he was going to be tortured slowly to death – and that any safewords or similar communication would have been perceived by his "torturer" as a sign of weakness, so all he dared do was turn his head and hope that if it really was still me, I'd notice.

Unfortunately, most of the signs that something has gone wrong can, under other circumstances or with other bottoms, be signs that everything is going exactly *right*: some bottoms love to cry in scene, and a bottom who's left his or her body in bliss acts pretty much like one who's withdrawn in terror. So to find out what's going on, you have to ask.

First, try one of the check-ins we mentioned in the previous chapter. If your bottom can't or won't respond, you should probably assume that s/he's in trouble.

Your strategy now will be a stronger version of the decompression you use at the end of a scene. First, get out of role yourself - your bottom doesn't need a schoolmistress right now, s/he needs a friend. Quickly and calmly remove any bondage or restraints; find out if s/he wants any scene symbols such as collars removed - some bottoms want them off right away, while others may feel rejected and abandoned if you remove them. Make sure s/he is physically warm - being wrapped in a cozy blanket feels very good to someone who's feeling emotionally chaotic.

Then, just put your arms around your partner and wait. Don't try to initiate conversation at first unless s/he seems to want to talk; let your bottom come back from whatever scary or angry or sad place s/he's in at an appropriate pace. It may be difficult at this point to suppress your own need for reassurance - you may, quite understandably, be feeling scared and guilty - but now isn't the time to take care of you, it's the time to take care of your bottom. (Later, when s/he is feeling better, you can get some support for yourself.)

As the bottom starts to come back, s/he may want to talk about what went wrong, or s/he may just want to be taken care of some more. Supplying a snack to elevate blood sugar and a beverage to rehydrate is very smart. S/he might want to be put to bed to sleep off the stress of the freak-out, or to soak in a nice warm bath.

In a few cases, the bottom may have gone into an angry enough place that s/he isn't able to accept touch or conversation or nurturing from you at all. This will probably be *very* difficult for you to handle without tapping into anger or defensiveness of your own. Listen quietly or leave the room for a while if necessary and let your bottom work through the anger solo; don't push limits here. After a while, you can check in and see if s/he is calmed down a bit and ready to accept some help from you.

It is possible that an emotional mishap in scene may open up an old wound that is deep enough to require professional help from a therapist. While we do not believe that you have an obligation to help with the financial burdens of such therapy, we think it's appropriate for you to be as emotionally supportive as possible for a friend who is doing this difficult work. And if it's *your* old wound that opened, we hope you have the honesty, courage and self-love to find the support you need for your own healing.

Aftershocks (Not the Seismic Kind)

When you return to everyday awareness after a scene, you could get a little shocked. What did you just do? Was it all right? Many tops experience feelings of guilt, shame and horror that we could get so turned on, and so satisfied, by doing such awful things. You may need to reassure yourself that you are really an okay person, and that you have perfectly functional boundaries to your dark side. Let your bottom help you with this: s/he, after all, is eroticized to your nastiness, and in a good position to reassure you that the scene was consensual, safe, satisfying to the bottom, and just plain hot.

Anywhere from a few minutes to a day or two after a big scene, you could experience "top drop." You may feel down in the dumps, inadequate, like maybe the scene really wasn't as hot as you thought it was - sometimes being a successful top can pose a major challenge to the maintenance of low self-esteem, so whatever part of you is responsible for maintaining your self-doubt may feel a need to be heard. You may find yourself questioning your sanity, tearing your scene apart with a tremendously critical eye, or convincing yourself that your bottom was just being polite when s/he was swooning in ecstasy. Or you may just feel kind of used up, low and tired.

This happens to a lot of us (it happens to bottoms, too, in a different way), so think of it like postpartum depression: you were just really high, so now the pendulum has swung the other way... and it will get back to the middle soon, really it will. This might be a good time to remind yourself of your respect for limits and safety, and to call your bottom or any other friend for a little reassurance.

Coming out of a role that is in any way parental (and how many top roles are not?) may be particularly difficult, as you may wake up internalized messages from your actual parents. When you get self-critical you may feel like a little kid who did something wrong - which makes it harder to stay centered, grounded and empowered.

Occasionally playing parents or bullies can open up old stuff inside you that you may not even remember having buried years ago. Memories and feelings from childhood traumas can cause particular problems, manifesting as memories you never had before, or recollections of body sensations, or disturbing dreams. If this starts happening to you, consider finding a good therapist. When events in the present open up fossilized conflicts, we all perceive this as confusing, painful or perhaps frightening. Please remember that when old wounds open it means a buried part of ourselves is now available to our consciousness, so there is an opportunity to know ourselves better and reclaim parts of ourselves we may have had to abandon long ago... to heal.

Physical Mishaps

Unless you have aim like Annie Oakley's and you play only with bottoms who are in perfect physical health, it is reasonable to be prepared for physical problems to come up during your scene. These may range from strokes that land off-target or clamps that get placed on nerves to heart attacks and seizures.

If the physical problem is due to a mistake of yours, the way to handle it depends on the flavor of the scene you're playing. It's imperative that you acknowledge the mistake somehow - if the bottom thinks you're not aware that you goofed, s/he will start to wonder what else you're not noticing, and to withdraw trust from you.

If you're simply exploring sensations together, there's nothing at all wrong with saying "Oops!" or "Sorry!" But if you're supposed to be an all-knowing mistress or a terrifying interrogator, this won't cut it. Sometimes, simply putting your hand on the place where the mistake happened and giving a quick comforting rub is enough to let the bottom know that you're aware things didn't feel the way they were supposed to. If you're playing a really mean role, you might try a phrase like "Yes, that *did* hurt, didn't it?" (Maniacal laughter is optional.)

If you make too many mistakes, or they're too serious, the bottom may want to stop the scene - and who can blame him or her? Spend a lot of time with this bottom deciding how to process your mistakes and whether or not to use this technique again, today or ever. Then get in a lot of practice time with the technique, on yourself or on an inanimate object, so you can do better next time.

If the mistake is such that it requires first aid, don't try to stay in role - stop the scene and get your first aid kit. The two of you can decide together whether or not to resume the scene from where you left off.

Remember, the unwritten contract you make when you agree to top someone is that you will take care of his or her well-being as well as your own for the duration of the scene - if s/he gets sick or hurt, you're in charge, and good tops take that responsibility seriously. Very occasionally, you will encounter a genuine physical emergency in your scene: more common ones include nausea and/or vomiting, faints and falls; less common ones (thank heavens!) include seizures and heart attacks. A responsible top is prepared for these emergencies.

Don't put someone into standing bondage unless you know how you would get them down if they became faint - this is not too rare an occurrence; panic snaps and winches help. Keep appropriate shears, scissors or a knife at arm's reach so that you can cut a sick person out of his or her bondage in no more than 30 seconds to a minute. Know the location and phone number of your nearest emergency room. We also strongly encourage you to get proper first aid and cardiopulmonary resuscitation training. Some major urban areas offer pervert-only first aid and CPR training, but if yours doesn't, contact the Red Cross and take one or more of their regular classes.

Outside-world emergencies. We know of one scene in which the top, a professional dominant, had her client tied in elaborate spider-web bondage to a table, with a big glass mirror suspended overhead so he could see his own helplessness. Both the top and the bottom shortly had the opportunity to explore more helplessness than they'd bargained for - the Loma Prieta earthquake hit, the mirror began to lurch back and forth, and the lights went out. (Both of them got out okay - but we hear that the pro-domme's playroom now features a Mylar mirror overhead, a blackout light in the outlet, and a pair of paramedic shears hanging on the wall.)

The outside world doesn't always cooperate with your desire for a quiet, intense, uninterrupted scene, and a competent top is aware that reality sneaks up on us in unpredictable ways. Outside-world problems range from interruptions by non-scene folks - kids, parents, housemates, neighbors and so on - through "acts of god/dess" like fires, storms, earthquakes and power outages.

If your scene gets interrupted by a person, some quick explanations are in order. A child who walks in on his or her parents' scene can often be reassured with a comparison to childhood games such as cowboys and Indians. The neighborhood cop, however, may need some serious briefing on basic standards of consent, and a lot of assurance that what s/he's seeing isn't abusive or assaultive behavior. Kidnap and similar scenes occasionally get interrupted by well-meaning onlookers - try to do your scene in a way that avoids this problem, since you don't want someone genuinely attacking you thinking they're heroically saving your bottom from criminal assault.

If the interruption is on a less personal basis - say, Hurricane Dora - you'll have to think and act fast and accurately. Be prepared to undo bondage, and have clothing available for yourself and your bottom. Your playroom should contain basic emergency equipment: a fire extinguisher, a smoke alarm, a first aid kit, a "blackout light" (a light designed to turn on during power outages), and a flashlight, at minimum. Having this equipment is an essential part of being a responsible top - remember, your bottom has entrusted his or her well-being to you.

11. Toys

Tops' toy collections can range from nothing at all - it's possible to do excellent S/M using nothing but your body and your imagination - through vast accumulations occupying several rooms of a household. Choosing toys that are appropriate to your play style and level of experience is a craft in itself; a classic novice top's error is to choose hideous nasty vicious toys that no bottom in his or her right mind would let a novice use.

In cookbooks, kitchen equipment is known as the "batterie de cuisine": a beginning cook is given a list of tools and supplies to start with, and a supplementary list of stuff to acquire later on for the master chef. We will do the same.

A Basic Toy Selection

These basic toys are a "starter set"; we think they're the best tools to go out and buy as you begin your toy collection. Very few of them are likely to cost you more than $40 or so, and if you're on a budget, you can often figure out less expensive alternatives that you can create from household supplies or find at the thrift store, supermarket or hardware store. So, to get you started, we recommend:

- **Rope.** Choose something soft, washable and at least $3/8$" thick; finish the ends with a piece of tape or stitch them with thread so they won't fray. Some folks swear by cotton magician's rope or soft nylon rope from the hardware store. Marine supply stores offer an enormous selection of excellent rope in different sizes, textures and colors. If

you're just getting started, try twelve-foot lengths of several different kinds and experiment with which you like best. Once you settle on one or two kinds, you'll probably want at least four twelve-foot lengths as well as a couple of shorter or longer lengths once you learn more about what kinds of bondage you like to do.

- **Restraints.** Unless you're very clever with knots, you'll find that a set of bondage cuffs for the wrists, and ideally a second set for the ankles, are a good investment. Try them on yourself before buying; tug the rings in all different directions to see if anything digs in or chafes, or if the cuff twists out of shape. Leather is nice if you can afford it, but there are good cuffs of nylon webbing which are strong and cheap. We don't recommend handcuffs or metal cuffs for beginners.

- **Blindfold.** The blindfold is a toy of such astonishing virtue that we had to set aside some space to talk about it. A blindfold can be a folded scarf or an elastic bandage, a nightshade from the drugstore or an elaborate leather mask from the toy store: no matter, they all work great.

  To understand the power of the blindfold, try one on yourself. Feel the change in your state of consciousness, how quiet you become when you take away the busy distractions of sight, how your consciousness moves away from the verbal entrainment of thought, how time passes in an easy flow in the trance of sensory deprivation.

  It is a powerful act to take away someone's vision, to make them helpless, to make them dependent on you for most kinds of functioning. You can accentuate this feeling by taking your blindfolded bottom for a walk, or sending him or her to the bathroom in the darkness. Stay nearby, don't let your bottom fall.

  There are practical advantages to blindfolding your bottom: then s/he can't see you fumble with the toys, or grab a clip to get your hair out of your eyes. We know a top who wears six-inch heels to tower over her bottoms, which she removes as soon as they can't see her anymore. So the blindfold offers privacy to the top, and relieves the bottom of the distractions of dealing with the material world. (We do recommend that you check with your bottom before slipping on a blindfold, particularly if the two of you are new to one another - some bottoms find them too threatening for first-time play.)

Blindfolds help to focus the bottom on what you are doing. Be aware that when you take away one sense, all others become accentuated. The blindfolded bottom will listen carefully, trying to figure out what you are going to do next - you can make this harder by playing music, or making noises on purpose to awaken his or her imagination.

Touch becomes much more intense for the blindfolded. Many tops try to maintain physical contact with a hand or a leg touching some part of the bottom's body at all times during the scene, while others may step back and let the bottom feel the abandonment of being blind and out of contact. Don't withdraw touch by accident - this is a powerful stimulus, and you want to stay purposeful with it. Don't leave a blindfolded person alone in a room where you can't watch over him or her.

Dossie recalls a scene at the first all-woman play party in San Francisco, where four tops requested her assistance because their bottom had gone all ticklish and couldn't stop giggling. Blindfold to the rescue! The bottom calmed down right away, and so did all her nervous tops.

We love blindfolds. Blindfolds are wonderful. Get one now.

- **Collar.** If you're really not interested in role-playing, you can skip this one, but we've found that many bottoms appreciate being collared as a way to start the scene and to go into bottom space. A nice dog collar from the pet store doesn't cost much. 20" seems to work out about right unless you play with very large or muscular people.

- *Clips and clamps.* Wooden clothespins from the hardware store, or plastic ones from the Asian grocery, are one of the cheapest, most versatile toys available. As a novice, you probably won't need more than six or so, although some advanced players enjoy playing with dozens or even hundreds of clamps. Clamps can go just about anywhere you can pinch up a fold of skin - breasts, chests, arms, legs, genitals, buttocks, backs and more (not near the eyes, please).

- *Candles.* Hot wax offers a relatively safe way to explore some intense sensations. Use only plain white paraffin candles to start with - dyes and scents raise the melting temperature and can make the wax too hot for many bottoms. As a rule of thumb, the softer the candle, the cooler the melting point of the wax. Beeswax has a skin-burningly high melting point and should be avoided. An ice cube used alternately with dribbles of hot wax can create very interesting sensations.

- *A soft flogger.* This is almost certainly going to be your biggest investment - but we find that more bottoms enjoy this sensation than any other, so if you can manage the $100-$150 such a toy is likely to cost, we encourage you to make the purchase. Shop at a store with clerks who can help you make a good selection. Try it on your thigh or arm, both softly and forcefully; you want something that gives a caressing, thuddy sensation, without too much sting or harshness. (You may want to add meaner whips to your collection later.) Soft floggers are often made of suede, deerskin, elk, cabretta or buffalo hide. If you're poor, you can make an adequate soft flogger by folding several lengths of soft rope in half, binding them together at the fold with tape or knots, and unraveling the ends, or by cutting strips from a discarded garment of soft suede or leather and folding them the same way. Practice on a pillow, comforter or plush toy until you can consistently land the tips of the tails - the nastiest part - exactly where you aim them.

- *A slapper or jockey bat.* If you're only going to choose one toy for smacking (as opposed to flogging), we think it should be either a leather slapper - a two-layered paddle made of stiff but flexible leather, which makes a very loud cracking noise but is unlikely to cause damage - or the short, broad-tipped riding crop called a "jockey bat." In our opinion, the jockey bat looks hotter but the slapper feels better. Both are easy to control and give a sensation that many bottoms enjoy. If you use the jockey bat, hit with the tip only. Both toys are available in riding stores for $10 or so.

- *Sex toys.* If you want to get yourself and/or your bottom off, a good vibrator is a worthwhile investment. We prefer the plug-in or rechargeable kinds because their vibration is much stronger. When you play with bottoms who enjoy being vaginally or anally penetrated, you may want to add a dildo and/or butt plug as well.

- *Safer sex supplies.* Unless you're in a completely and consistently monogamous relationship, you should be putting latex or other barriers over anything that comes into contact with blood, semen, vaginal fluid, urine, feces and any other body fluids. Experiment with condoms until you find the ones you like; you may want some lubricated ones for penetration play and some unlubed ones for oral play. (Dossie's definition of a gentleman is a man who has masturbated with a condom on for a month or two so he *knows* how to make it work.) Get latex gloves in your size. Use dental dams or plastic wrap if you perform cunnilingus or have it performed on you. Try different water-based lubricants to see which you like; we recommend lubes containing nonoxynol-9 or one of its variants, octoxynol-9, nonoxynol-15 and so on (some people are allergic to one or more, so experiment cautiously at first). You may want to use a thinner, runnier lube for vaginal play and a thicker, gooier one for anal play. If you play with inserting a real penis into a vagina or anus, consider purchasing spermicidal suppositories which you can insert to help kill sperm and/or virus if your condom fails. If you are unsure about how any of these safer sex supplies are used, contact your local AIDS hotline for more information.

- *Emergency supplies.* Your basic toy kit should contain a pair of heavy-duty shears such as paramedic's shears, or a blunt-tipped sharp knife that can be run under rope or restraints without poking the bottom's skin. You will also need to think about dealing with power outages, and many dungeons are dark, so keep a flashlight handy.

More Advanced Toys

As you learn more about play technique in general and your own specific style, you will probably want to acquire more toys. Here are some of the ones we like:

Helplessness toys. You can make your partner helpless with anything from pretend bondage ("put your wrists behind your back and keep them there until I say you can move them") through elaborate and expensive harnesses and body bags.

You can learn a lot about what kinds of helplessness you enjoy by experimenting with soft rope. If you find yourself attaching your partner's wrists to his or her thighs over and over again, you might want to acquire a set of restraints made especially for that position. If a bottom with arms pulled tightly back and chest thrust forward turns you on (and you play with people flexible enough to sustain this difficult position), a "mono-glove" that laces arms together behind backs might be a good investment. Posture collars hold the head high and restrict head and shoulder movement... yum. A field trip to your local leather emporium, or a delightful evening spent browsing through one of the good mail order catalogs, will yield up many such tantalizing possibilities (save up your pennies!).

You can also make your partner helpless by taking away some of his or her senses. Blindfolds, as we noted earlier, boost sensation and sharpen focus. Earplugs cost almost nothing and help muffle sound (although they don't block it entirely); adding heavy earmuffs of the kind worn by airline ground crews, or audio headphones of the kind you may already own, blocks sound out even more. Hoods of spandex or leather encase the entire head, taking away the bottom's sight, smell, much of his or her hearing, even the feel of air currents on the face.

Gags require special care in selection - a too-large gag can leave a bottom with a sore jaw, or even choke him or her if it holds the mouth open too far for comfortable swallowing. The part that goes into the mouth *must* be firmly attached to the part that goes around the head so the bottom cannot swallow or inhale it. Catherine prefers a gag that absorbs saliva, such as a square scarf folded diagonally with a large firm knot tied in the middle. Other tops like ball gags (many commercial ones are too large for the mouths of smaller bottoms, so you may have to make your own) or "bit"-type gags that place a leather bar in the bottom's mouth. No gag can stop a bottom from making any noise at all - grunts and muffled screams will still emerge, so don't count on your gag enabling you to do heavy pain play while Mom dozes lightly in the next room.

For complete helplessness and immobilization, many tops like to use some combination of kitchen-type plastic wrap or pallet wrap, plus sticky tape and, perhaps, a few sports bandages. With these few simple supplies, you can mummify a bottom so firmly that s/he can't move a muscle and can't even feel his or her own skin. (Dehydration is a danger here - give your bottom water with a sports bottle or baby bottle, and don't play this game in an overly warm or cold room.) Cut holes - carefully - with a small pair of sharp scissors so you can get to the bottom's skin in those special places.

You may want to add some things for attaching people *to* in your bedroom or play space. An old-fashioned four-poster or brass bed is "deniable" and useful. Eye-bolts in ceilings and walls can be explained away as "for plant hangers" when the folks come to visit (if you're not absolutely certain of your ability to center an eye-bolt in a joist or stud, get professional help). Ottomans and "kneeling chairs" convert readily into spanking horses, and a little imagination and carpentry will enable you to create bondage equipment that can be shoved into a closet or under the bed when you're not playing.

Of course, the more helpless you make your bottom, the more responsible you are for his or her well-being. If your bottom is in bondage, don't go out of earshot; if s/he's gagged as well, don't leave the room. When you've made someone as helpless as an infant, take care of him or her as carefully as you would an infant.

Toys for hitting. Oooh, our favorites. Striking toys can be found in the supermarket, the hardware store, the stationery store, antique stores, tack shops - even, if you're feeling perverse, leather stores.

Things that are basically broad, stiff and flat fall under the general subcategory of "paddles." Paddles are most often made of leather, which is relatively flexible and stingy, or of wood, which is stiff and more thuddy (although the sting-to-thud ratio of any striking toy depends mostly on its proportion of weight to breadth). Hairbrushes, a traditional spanking implement, are basically small paddles. If you prowl antique stores you can sometimes find old fraternity paddles, which are vicious, or novelty paddles with corny sayings on them, which are embarrassing. Make sure your paddle has no harsh edges or corners which can cut or abrade. Paddles with holes are hot to look at and hurt a lot, and are far more likely to break skin than smooth paddles.

Long flat flexible striking toys fall under the broad category of "straps." It's relatively easy to find good straps outside leather stores - an old, soft, well-worn, broad leather belt from the '60s is a thrift store treasure. Tack shops and antique stores (watch for leather razor strops in good condition) are also good places to find straps. The sound of a top pulling his or her belt out of its loops and doubling it up is delightfully scary. But be extra-cautious in negotiating play with straps - they are commonly used by abusive parents and spouses, and are thus likelier than other toys to trigger flashbacks to nonconsensual violence.

You'll hear multi-tailed toys called "cats," "cat-o-nine-tails," "flails" and other names; we'll call them, generically, "floggers." Floggers may have just a few tails (if there are only two, they're usually called "quirts") or hundreds. They are most commonly made of leather, but we've seen nice ones made of rope, rubber and manmade materials as well. Braided tails are nasty, tails with knots nastier yet. Some floggers are made of the gentlest, most caressing suede or deerskin, others of tough harsh hide. Try a potential flogger on yourself - or, better yet, have a trusted friend give you some strokes with it - before you buy it if possible, and certainly before you use it on somebody else.

Long thin stiff rods fall under the category of "canes." Bottoms mostly either love canes fanatically or hate them passionately - they hurt a lot, and the pain comes in two waves, one when the cane strikes, and another a few moments later when the tissue decompresses. Classically, canes are made of rattan, often varnished. Rattan canes feel wonderful, but are hard to clean if they come in contact with blood, plasma or other body fluids - so we also often use canes made of manmade materials like fiberglass and Delrin. Cane sluts (like us) like to have several of each kind, in various lengths, breadths, and flexibilities.

Bullwhips, blacksnakes and signal whips are called "single-tailed whips," and are for use only by genuine experts. The "crack" these whips can make is actually the sound of the tip breaking the sound barrier - that's how fast they travel, and how dangerous they can be. A single-tailed whip can tear flesh. If you haven't practiced assiduously on inanimate objects for a long time, don't even think about using one on a human being.

Toys for pinching. While you can do perfectly wonderful S/M with nothing but a bag of wooden clothespins, players who love the slow build-up and cathartic release of wearing and removing clamps often collect many different kinds (one bottom we know has a box the size of a small suitcase that contains nothing but clips and clamps). The classic place to apply clamps is on the nipples, but a fair percentage of bottoms find that particular type of pain difficult to handle (others adore it, so you have to ask). Clamps also work well just about anywhere on the body where you can grab a pinch of skin and slip on a clamp. Occasionally a clamp gets put on a place that is truly intolerable (perhaps on top of a nerve); it is entirely reasonable for a bottom to ask to have such a clamp moved, maybe only half an inch or so. Some clamps, such as Japanese clovers, tighten when you pull on them. Others have teeth or ridges that bite.

One thing that all clamps have in common is that they hurt the most coming off, and the longer they've been on, the more they hurt on removal - be prepared for a yelp or jump from your bottom. Plan your timing; clamp removal after orgasm is *much* harder to handle. If you're being nice, remove the clamp gently and gradually... if you're being mean (and if it's not toothed or ridged), yank it off. You can also string several non-toothed clamps at intervals along a cord so that you can yank them all off at once - this is called a "zipper," and delivers a serious jolt of pain and a major flood of endorphins.

Toys for poking. Poky feelings may come from something sharp being pressed into the skin, or from something sharp actually being pressed *through* the skin.

If you don't want to break skin, bamboo skewers (like for shish kabob) poke beautifully - a blindfolded bottom may think you're piercing him or her (fun for mindfuck). A Wartenburg wheel, used by neurologists, is a small wheel with very sharp spokes on the end of a handle; you run it along the skin like a pizza cutter. Yeowch!

Play that actually breaks skin is to be done *only* by experienced tops or under the supervision of an experienced top. Play piercings, typically done with disposable hypodermic needles or sterilized acupuncture needles, involve inserting needles just below the surface of the skin and back out again - not for the permanent insertion of jewelry, but just for the sensation of being pierced. Cuttings, properly placed no deeper

113

than a cat scratch, are usually done with a sterile scalpel. Some players rub ash or tattoo ink into a decorative cutting to make a permanent mark.

Toys that heat or cool. Temperature offers a powerful range of sensations. We mentioned hot wax and ice cubes earlier, but they're worth noting again here, since they're such simple and versatile toys. A bottom may find it impossible to distinguish between extreme heat and extreme cold - we've heard of scenes in which a top convinces a blindfolded bottom that s/he's about to be branded, then presses an ice cube into his or her flesh.

Some folks enjoy playing with "chemical heat" from spicy oils like cinnamon or peppermint, or from commercial concoctions like Ben Gay or Tiger Balm. It takes only a tiny bit of any of these to create a strong sensation, particularly on mucous membranes like cunts or assholes - start with the tiniest dab, and give the heat several minutes to build before you consider adding more. If you use too much and your bottom can't handle it, apply a lot of anything oily - vaseline, cold cream, even vegetable oil or butter from the kitchen - to the affected area to dilute the chemical, then send your victim to the shower to suds it off with shampoo.

The ultimate temperature play is branding. Like piercing and cutting, branding is to be done only by very experienced tops. The way it's done on TV westerns, or in "The Story of O," does *not* work on people-hide the way it does on cowhide - learn from an expert before you even consider exploring branding.

Toys that zap. Electricity play is a fairly specialized play style with some special risks. The impulses that tell your bottom's heart when to beat are electrical, and you most definitely do not want to confuse those impulses - so a general rule for electricity play is "never above the waist" (and *never*, of course, from one nipple to the other). We also think it's better not to do electricity play with a bottom who has a heart condition, and to be cautious about using it on or near piercings.

114

Within those rules, though, there is still room for fun. Some manufacturers have created electrical units for scene play with specialized attachments, butt plugs and cock rings and such; these are a big investment but very pleasant to play with. Relaxacisors (a quackish weight-loss gadget from the '40s and '50s) deliver a stronger sensation. Stun guns and cattle prods are extremely strong, too much so for most players - we don't recommend them unless your bottom is in good health and both of you have had lots of experience with less intense forms of electricity play.

A special case is the "violet wand" - yet another medical device, once thought to help with such problems as baldness. The violet wand delivers electricity in a different form that stays on the surface of the skin rather than going into deeper tissues, so it's generally considered safer for use above the waist (although you should keep it away from the eyes and from any piercings, pacemakers or prostheses). The sensation feels a bit like the shock you get from walking across a wool carpet and touching a doorknob, except it goes on and on and.... Again, a big investment, but the folks who love these *really* love them.

Toys for turning on and getting off. While many people do S/M without genital sex, we're strong advocates for having as much sex as possible - so our toy collections tend to include lots of gadgets for getting people aroused and giving them orgasms.

Dildoes and butt plugs give bottoms (and tops!) that wonderful filled-up feeling that makes orgasms so much more worthwhile. Assholes in particular do not take well to being harshly stretched - insert plugs and such only after plenty of preparatory finger play, v-e-r-y gradually and gently, and don't go for the Guinness book on plug size unless you know your bottom can handle it. Use lots and lots and lots and lots of lube (one top we know says "If there isn't lube dripping from the ceiling, you haven't used enough"). If anything burns or creates a sharp or tearing pain, stop immediately - either fix the situation that's causing the pain, or move on to another activity. Butt toys need to have a wide flange at the bottom so they don't get lost in the rectum - a lost toy is at best uncomfortable and embarrassing, and at worst a serious emergency.

Vaginas are less picky about what gets inserted in them (although scrupulous cleanliness is essential for anything that goes into a vagina). Still, the sensation of being hurt or bumped deep inside is not erotic to most women. We suggest that if you like to play with dildoes and other insertables, you acquire a few different sizes and shapes, and keep track of which bottoms like which - or, better yet, encourage your bottoms to own their own dildoes that are exactly the size and shape they like (and that get used only on them).

Toys can give you genitals other than the ones nature gave you. If you have a vagina, you can strap on a penis (or insert one into yourself and still have one left over for a friend). If you want a bigger or harder penis, open the drawer and take one out. Ever wish you had a penis on your leg, or your face? Or that you could have two penises, one for each hole? Use your imagination - and your MasterCard.

Own lots of lube. Yes, good water-based lube is expensive - but you paid more for that half-gallon of premium ice cream you polished off last week, and we bet you didn't enjoy it half as much. Lube is important for good sex and essential for good safer sex. Don't be stingy.

Toys for role-playing. For tops and bottoms, every day can be Halloween. Role-playing doesn't have to involve specialized toys or costumes - imagination and creativity can certainly suffice - but we think half the fun of a role-playing scene is the trip to the thrift store beforehand. (Well, maybe a quarter of the fun.)

If you play with one role a lot, you may want to consider getting toys, props and costumes appropriate to that role. Daddies may wear big threatening leather belts. Bitch goddesses lace themselves into shiny tight corsets and spike-heeled shoes. Interrogators and rapists hide their features with masks or hoods. Pirates wear high boots and dashing shirts. Schoolmistresses have long frumpy skirts and high-necked

117

blouses and whippy scary canes. If you like to train puppies, you'll need collars and bowls and rolled-up newspapers; if you prefer ponies, get some bridles and crops and maybe an insertable tail or two.

Your role-playing costumes and props serve a dual function: they help you and your bottoms get into the mood when you're actually playing, and they signal your particular role interest to potential bottoms. So get yourself over to the thrift store or costume shop and have fun!

Toys for the Road

Unless you're prepared to haul a steamer trunk along to every play date (and some tops do exactly that), you'll probably want to think about developing a portable toy kit.

Of course, "portable" is relative. Both of us usually use a softball bag from the sporting goods store for carrying our toys to parties and demonstrations. But we also like to be able to drop a few small toys into our purses, just in case.

One player we know uses a small zippered bag, about 8" x 10" x 2", for his portable toybag. It contains a couple of lengths of rope, a mini-whip made of four leather thongs folded in half and rubber-banded together at the fold (which can also be disassembled if he or his partner wants to use the thongs individually), and a few clothespins. Safer sex is taken care of with several latex gloves in his size, a few condoms and some individual-sized packets of lubricant. Emergency supplies include a small flashlight and a pair of paramedic's shears. There's still plenty of room left over for whatever specialized small equipment he wants for any particular session - a lightweight collar, a small tube of hot cream, a mini-vibrator, a cock ring or whatever.

If you're traveling by air - and especially through customs - you'll have to do some serious thinking about what to take with you. For domestic travel, bags that get checked through as luggage aren't inspected closely - you'll have to balance the potential embarrassment of having your carry-on toys inspected at the metal detector against the possibility of the airline losing your luggage. (Important note: The airline will *not* allow you to carry on anything that you could possibly use to assault a passenger or hijack the plane. They are particularly firm about firearms, knives, handcuffs and chain/lock combinations.)

Customs agents for overseas travel may be very cool about your toys - or not. We've heard some scary stories. If you're traveling to a very conservative or sex-negative country, we think you should probably stick to toys that have real-world uses: clothesline, clothespins, hairbrushes, belts, candles and so on. Consider shipping any toys you buy overseas home separately. If you have a friendly travel agent, s/he may be able to advise you further about whether you're likely to get hassled.

Maintaining Toys

Well-maintained toys are clean, free of breakage or flaws, and a joy to use. Poorly maintained toys can cause injury and spread disease, and signal to the world that you're a sloppy top who doesn't care about your bottoms. You probably wouldn't go to a play date with dirty hair and smelly armpits; your toys deserve at least as much attention as your body does.

Any toy that you suspect has come into contact with body fluids needs to be cleaned. Rubber toys, metal toys and toys of manmade materials like silicon and plastic can be lightly handwashed using a cleanser like Hibiclens and warm water, then soaked for half an hour in a solution of one part household chlorine bleach to nine parts water. Leather toys should be cleaned using leather cleaner, left to air-dry for at least a day, then reconditioned, before being used on another bottom. (The exact technique will depend on the type of leather; check with the store or craftsperson who sold it to you.) Toys made of plant materials like rattan and wood should be varnished if they are likely to come into contact with various bottoms' body fluids. If such a toy gets fluids on it, clean it thoroughly with nonoxynol-9-containing toy cleanser, or with soap and water and then a liberal wipe of hydrogen peroxide. If you suspect that

119

fluids may have gotten under the varnish, sand the varnish off, do the soap-water-peroxide thing, let it dry thoroughly, then re-varnish it.

Inspect all your toys frequently for cracks, weak spots, raveled stitching, etc. If you find a problem, fix it promptly (and if you don't have time right then, set the toy aside where it can't possibly get mixed up with the toys you use). If a toy can't be repaired, discard it.

Play-test bondage equipment and eye-bolts periodically by having someone heavy try them out. If something seems creaky or wobbly, fix it before you play with it again.

Some Final Thoughts on Toys

As the old saying goes, "Size doesn't matter" - toybag size, that is. No knowledgeable bottom judges a top on how many toys s/he has. Tops get judged on their skill, creativity, character and ethics, not on their stuff.

If you're a "gear queer" who enjoys collecting dozens or hundreds of cool toys, and you're not bankrupting yourself to do it, we applaud you - we love beautiful toys, own a lot ourselves, and have friends whose collections are practically museum-quality. (You're also helping to keep our leatherworker friends, a vital link in the community, busy creating instruments of joy.) But don't forget that your primary focus should be on your bottom, not your toys: s/he's bottoming to you, and that's exactly the way you want it, right?

12. So Where Are All the Bottoms?

If you ask a bunch of bottoms, you will hear heartfelt and often bitter complaints about the scarcity of tops in the S/M community. The good news (if you're a top) is that this is often true - particularly in heterosexual communities or those in smaller cities and rural environments. The bad news is that it's changing: both of us have noticed that more and more of the new young players coming into the scene are top-identified.

Dossie remembers that twenty years ago, in the pre-assertiveness-training women's community in which she came of age as a player, there essentially *were* no tops. So bottoms politely took turns topping one another so that everybody got to get played with - and thus got to learn about and appreciate the delights of running the show. Even now, there are more bottoms than tops in most communities - often many more.

What that means to you, particularly if you're a hetero-sexual female, a lesbian or a gay man, is that you as a top are in something of a buyer's market. That certainly doesn't mean, however, that all you have to do is lean back and casually choose from a parade of eager bottoms who are all dying to throw themselves at your feet. Quality tops get quality bottoms - it's up to you, not only to be a quality top, but to make sure your potential bottoms know it.

This goal is not accomplished by boasting about your true master- or mistress-hood, or by acting pushy and bossy outside scene space in order to demonstrate your natural gift for domination, or by hauling around a bunch of toys that you had to take out a second mortgage to buy. The best tops we know are quite modest, often soft-spoken, and always scrupulously polite - until they've finished their negotiations and the scene begins... then, watch out!

So, you ask, how do I let the world know of my wonderful toppiness without coming off like a cross between P.T. Barnum and Attila the Hun? The first suggestion we can make is that you learn as much as you possibly can, and never stop learning. Take classes. Read everything you can get your hands on (remembering, of course, to distinguish between fantasy/fiction and reality). Practice, practice, practice - if not on an eager subject, then on an inanimate object like a pillow or teddy bear, or on yourself.

Be a joiner. If you can, we strongly recommend that you join your local S/M club - not necessarily to find the bottom of your dreams (although this is certainly a possibility), but to gain friends, mentors and information. Many large urban communities have several clubs of different orientations (gay, lesbian, het, bi, male-top, female-top, pansexual and so on); pick one or several that suit your orientation - and if the only one you can find doesn't suit your orientation, get in touch with them and ask them what else is out there. This is an essential step in your development as a top and as a player, and an important way to give back to the community by helping to provide support for folks who are newer and scareder than you. If you don't have a local club, join one of the big urban ones (at least that way you'll get to read the newsletter, and perhaps to attend an event or two during vacation time), or start your own.

If you think you are too shy to go to an S/M support group, allow us to reassure you. Such meetings are nowhere near as threatening as you may imagine. The first Society of Janus meetings Dossie attended were held in the basement of a church: how wholesome. People at support group meetings are generally friendly and straightforward, not likely to come on with a lot of attitude or deeply in role, and what cruising there is is customarily civilized and respectful. Confidentiality is paramount - nobody is going to call up your boss or spouse and reveal your secret life, and if you run into someone from the office at the meeting... well, what is s/he doing there? And if your fantasy embarrasses you so much that you cannot imagine getting together in a room with other people who also have fantasies, remember that none of them can read your mind - so your privacy is ensured anyway.

It pays to advertise. When you're searching for play partners or life partners, what you are doing is marketing - and if you think it's beneath your toppish dignity to market yourself, we hope you and your dignity have many happy nights together.

The first step in marketing a product is, of course, to make sure that the product is marketable. Are you technically skilled? Are you responsible? Are you flexible? Are you empathetic? Do you take good care of your physical and emotional health? If you didn't answer all of these questions with an emphatic "yes," we suggest you do some close self-examination and self-improvement: all the marketing in the world won't move a product that people don't want.

Next, take a look at your packaging. While it's not necessary to wrap yourself in custom leather from head to toe, a little toppish accessorizing helps catch bottoms' attention. Gay men and lesbians can use hanky and key codes as shorthand to communicate their orientations and interests, which is convenient; unfortunately, these signifiers haven't worked their way very far into the het community just yet. Since many male bottoms are also fetishists, the wearing of fetish apparel - tall boots, tight corsets, leather skirts or pants - is convenient code by which het female tops can communicate their interests. Heterosexual male tops can run into problems - if they look too fetish-y, women may assume they are gay and discount them as possible play partners. Still, a leather vest over a handsome silk shirt or turtleneck sweater, possibly paired with leather pants, a "significant-looking" leather belt or a small whip worn on the left side, and/or a pair of shiny leather boots, will get your message across. Various kinds of drag - schoolmaster or -mistress, pirate, cowboy, cop - will, of course, get attention from devotees of all genders and orientations.

Get the word out. Techniques used by vanilla people for partner-finding - personal ads in print media, voice mail, or on the Internet or computer bulletin boards - can also be used to good advantage by kinky folk. Some of these venues may not allow overtly kinky ads, but a little clever indirectness can usually get your point across (words like "take-charge," "stern," "bossy" and so on, or references to favorite works of literature, are common routes). Others, deplorably, charge more for kinky ads than for vanilla ones. We suggest that you protest these policies when you find them, but if they're the only game in town, well, it's better to get the word out via a discriminatory newspaper than not to get the word out at all.

The trick to writing a good personal ad is to be as clear and specific as possible about your toppy interests while still communicating a good sense of what you're like as a person. This is true whether you're placing your own ad or responding to someone else's. (We recommend, by the way, that you do both.) One friend of ours says "The ideal personal ad gets exactly one response - the right one."

To cruise or not to cruise? We think singles-bar-type cruising - walking up to total strangers and asking "So, wanna get whipped?" - is probably not an optimal strategy for you, unless you're very gorgeous or very self-assured. (However, neither of us has ever been bold enough to try it, so we don't know for sure.)

If you try thinking of an S/M event as more like a cocktail party than a singles bar, though, your chances will go up. One of the more successful cruisers we know says he has a seldom-fail opening line: "Hi, I'm Mike."

While some bottoms choose tops who are bossy, pushy and overbearing, we believe that such bottoms are likely to have trouble separating their fantasies from their realities - not a good formula for a future of safe, life-enhancing play together. The bottoms we suggest you play with are the ones you connect with at a personal level - the folks with whom you "click" in terms of personality, intelligence and chemistry. And the best way to find out if that "click" is going to happen is to simply be yourself - personable, honest and interesting to talk to. If you do this right, there will be plenty of time to be mean, harsh and overbearing later, after the scene has begun.

The art of cruising comes at the moment when this friendly get-acquainted chatter turns to matters more personal. If you're at an S/M event, this isn't too difficult: simply ask "So, what kinds of play do you enjoy?" and begin discovering whether the two of you have enough in common for further discussion. (We don't suggest, by the way, that you push too hard for play that very evening. If you can get your potential bottom's phone number, or a date for coffee or a meal at some other time, that will give you more opportunity to get to know him or her, and will probably lead to better play later. On the other hand, if you're both interested in playing right then and there, and your negotiations show no deal-breakers, then why not?)

If you're at an event that is sexual but not specifically S/M in nature, we suggest you stay specific about the kinds of activities that interest you - "I'm into S/M" is a turnoff to a lot of people who have mistaken ideas about what that means, but "I enjoy bondage" or "I've had fun spanking some of my partners" might pique someone's interest.

If you're at a non-sexual event, you have to be even more indirect. A mild, flirtatious joke about "Oooh, you naughty boy" or "How come there's never a slave around when you want one?" or "She was all tied up that day... and I couldn't find the time to untie her" will give you some information about your potential partner's interests. If s/he flirts back, you can take the conversation onto a slightly more direct level, although we still suggest you avoid words like "S/M," "dominance," "submission" and "pain" until communication is established.

Introducing S/M Into an Existing Relationship

These tips are all very well for all those single tops out there, you say. But what if you're already happily coupled, and hoping to introduce your partner to the joys that lie within your delightfully toppish hands?

"So, honey, whaddaya say tonight I tie you up and flog you within an inch of your life?" is probably not a good start. Keep in mind that most people have a very inaccurate view of what S/M and its practitioners are all about. Thus, you might do better to open the discussion by talking about a specific and not-too-scary activity that interests you - a little light bondage, some mild role-playing or a bit of sensuous spanking are often good places to start. Some couples enjoy reading erotica aloud to one another as a way to get turned on, and explore actual play later as it starts to feel safe.

S/he may surprise you by greeting your proposal with enthusiasm. Or s/he may have some concerns, which it's important that you talk through. (Often, first-timers are more comfortable topping, not bottoming. You should probably go along with this plan if at all possible. Once s/he sees that what you have in mind is safe, exciting and fun, s/he may be more open to being on the receiving end.)

If s/he says "Absolutely not!" you're kind of stuck. You can try suggesting that s/he read some of the excellent literature listed in the Resource Guide at the back of this book in order to learn more (we recommend the how-to nonfiction, not the fictional erotica, which often depicts play so strong as to be extremely frightening to novices), and maybe even going together to a program put on by your local S/M club. But, let's face it, some people are just vanilla. If your partner turns out to be one of these, there's not much point in nagging: you will have to choose between opening up your relationship (which we encourage you to do honestly and consensually), giving up your interest in S/M, or giving up your partner. One of us has had to do the latter, and it is a sad and difficult decision which we hope you never have to make.

Choosing the Right Bottom

We know tops who have found lifelong joy, connection and pleasure with the right bottom - and tops who have been plunged into nightmares of guilt, self-doubt and depression by the wrong one.

We want you to be in the first group. So what characteristics should you look for in a bottom? We think these are
important:

- *Responsibility for one's own actions.* A bottom who
  blames you when anything goes wrong... or the obverse, a
  bottom who expects you to control all aspects of your scene,
  without any input or feedback... is not taking the proper
  amount of responsibility for his or her own actions. We
  know one bottom who, during his pre-scene negotiations,
  tells his tops, "I want you to know that I'm doing this scene
  with you because I want to, and because I trust you to take
  good care of me. If anything goes wrong, we'll work it out
  together; I won't lay it all on you." Not surprisingly, this
  bottom finds lots of play partners.

- *Ability to give as well as take.* Sometimes "do-me
  queens" don't give energy back simply because they don't
  know how to - that problem is easily fixed by telling them.
  But others feel entitled to simply lie back and get done,
  without any desire to make sure that your needs get met. If
  you feel that your bottom falls into the latter category, it's
  time for some serious renegotiation before you burn out
  badly.

- *Discretion.* It's always tempting to enjoy hearing gossip
  about your fellow players - but if you hear a bottom
  spreading bad rumors about his or her previous tops, you
  might want to ask yourself what s/he will say about you if
  the relationship ends. Watch out especially for the bottom
  who has nothing good to say about *any* of his or her former
  play partners.

- *Self-control.* A bottom with a reputation for bad-
  temperedness or intoxication is probably not a safe choice of
  partner. Remember, sooner or later you have to untie 'em.

- *Supportiveness.* Most bottoms will support you
  enthusiastically while you're acting like a top, especially if

you're acting like the kind of top they like. But a good bottom will also be supportive when you're not acting like a top - when you're feeling tired, vulnerable, confused, depressed or simply untoppy. Just as it's not much fun to be someone's "sex object" or "money object," it's hurtful to be thought of as a "pain object" - or, as Catherine says, "a life support system for a whip."

All of this - looking for and finding the right bottom - probably sounds like a lot of work. But we assure you, when s/he is looking up at you with that marvelous combination of fear, awe and love, all the work and struggle will recede into nothingness, and your bottom-finding time and energy will seem like the best investment you ever made.

13. Special Cases

Novices

Do you want to bring out S/M virgins? Topping a player who has little or no experience requires special care and commitment, and extra responsibility. The rewards are clear - a first-time fulfillment of years of fantasy can be incredibly exciting for both parties, hot stuff with heady feelings of conquest of the unspeakable. If the scene comes off well, your bottom will remember you with fond feelings forever, and you will feel like Santa Claus.

On the other hand, most often the first time we try anything, we don't do it as well as we will when we've had some opportunities to practice - so the first scene is often anticlimactic. Novice bottoms may have extreme fantasies but find that the realities are much harder to deal with than they thought, so be prepared to stop much sooner than you'd anticipated. Remember that the first time is probably not the last time... there's tons of stuff to learn to pull off your favorite fantasy, and you get as many tries as it takes.

What knowledge do you need to top an inexperienced bottom? If you are a novice top, and your bottom is also new to S/M, then go very, very slowly. You will both make lots of mistakes, and if you can accept that, you can learn from them. If you are the more experienced player, then remember that virgin bottoms will not know much about their limits, and will not know the consequences of various types of play. Dossie recalls:

> I once topped a novice bottom at a party, a sweet young thing all done up in white lace, eagerly waiting to be

decimated. I started slow, but this bottom liked the feel of it and worked all the way up to a heavy caning by the end of the scene. Afterward, it became apparent that she did not know that she would have bruises from such a caning, and that she had a vanilla lover at home – I will never forget to ask about marks again! I took care to drive her home, and call the next day to make sure she was all right – she was, thank goodness.

So when you top a novice bottom, be sure to ask lots of questions, so you will have the opportunity to fill in the bottom's information about what to expect. Many first scenes are, rightly, very lightweight - it is inappropriate to push limits hard when you are topping a novice. Rather, you should be prepared to be very supportive, and share in the excitement of doing something that is new for the bottom, even if you've done it before. After all, good play is not judged by how heavy it is, but rather by how wonderful it feels.

Other bottoms may go so far out in a first scene as to push the limits of experienced tops (never underestimate the power of endorphins). A friend of ours describes a scene in which he was asked to top a novice whose stated purpose was to satisfy her intellectual curiosity about S/M so she could write about it.

Our friend started out cautiously, but the bottom turned out to have an enormous pain tolerance, so soon she was wearing sixteen small but very intense clamps on her skin, and liking it a lot, and the top was starting to feel like his limits were being pushed. He removed the clamps, and spent half an hour doing various other things. Toward the end, she was kneeling at his feet and he saw a shadow pass over her face. He asked: "Is there something you want to tell me?" "Yes, Master," she replied. "You may speak." "Please, Sir, the clamp you left on my clit is beginning to hurt a little."

New players need and deserve a supportive environment in which to explore S/M and to learn how to bottom. Good tops honor and value the trust and hard work a new bottom offers to us when s/he struggles with a new sensation, or fulfills a role s/he has never played before. We can help by presenting new events one at a time, by giving novices plenty of opportunities to feel their way into an unfamiliar sensation or command, and by letting them find out what they like and don't like without fear of judgment or condemnation.

When we watch over our novice bottoms carefully, and treat them with responsibility and respect, we get to share in the great adventure of starting down the path of S/M exploration, and to witness the blossoming of many happy little sluts and slaves.

Professional Domination

The world of professional domination is one of the highest accomplishments of the S/M scene. A good professional dominant is a skilled and respected expert on many if not all forms of S/M. Many give their knowledge back to the community by teaching classes or workshops, as well as being available for actual play in negotiated sessions.

The professional dominant's studio can be an amazing site to behold. Entire houses may be full of rooms decorated and furnished to satisfy every S/M fantasy, with much of the furniture offering practical applications for play: racks for bondage, horses for bend-over beatings, overhead winches to support the standing bottom for a flogging, specially designed bondage tables for the most complete immobilization. Many professional studios include rooms for different fantasies: the dungeon, all black and chains... the nursery for big babies, with lots of flannel and extra-large teddy bears... transformation rooms, with costumes, wigs and makeup to turn the bottom into the creature of his or her fantasy... white rooms with examining tables for playing Doctor or Nurse Nasty.

Paying for the opportunity to play with such an expert is considered completely acceptable by S/M community standards. A person may want to see a professional because s/he wants to learn from an expert - a top who is somewhat uncomfortable with bottoming but wants to learn from that experience can often arrange a scene with a professional that includes exactly what s/he wants in a confidential environment. A bottom may go to a professional dominant for elaborate scenes that s/he can't get from his or her partner. A bottom who loves his wife and kids, their house in the suburbs and his standing in a straight community can visit a professional occasionally without giving up the rest of his life. And money is a fair and clean exchange for fantasy play sculpted by an expert to the bottom's needs, even when the bottom needs to serve. Some professionals also offer submissives, or switch themselves, for carefully negotiated and limited scenes with customers they trust (for obvious reasons of safety, there are few professional bottoms advertising in the open market).

A competent professional dominant is good at limits and boundaries. S/he will know which fantasies are workable in a professional relationship and which are not. It is traditional in professional scenes to include a lot of extremely wild S/M and to exclude actual sex, partly because that may fit better for the professional, and mostly because the exchange of sex for money is illegal in most states.

If you would like to know more about the world of professional domination, we recommend the excellent and hilarious English film "Personal Services," very loosely based on the career of British dominatrix Cynthia Payne, which includes wonderful depictions of parties and Christmas dinner at her house of pain.

Virtual S/M

A tribute to the dedication and ingenuity of the modern nerd, computer bulletin boards and communication networks are now bustling with sex talk, a good source of information as well as a way to play with other people. Virtual S/M is actual play done by computer, similar to phone sex except you can't hear the heavy breathing. (As we write this, various government bills are being proposed which, if passed, will limit this form of play severely. Write your representative and demand your right to communicate freely.)

There are two basic forms of play on the computer: e-mail correspondence and real-time. In correspondence, which you can also do by regular mail, the top sends instructions to the bottom, who acts on those instructions and then reports back to the top on the experience. Instructions might be real acts, like go to the supermarket and pick out the largest carrot you can find, caress and lick it in the market without getting caught, or they could be fantasies, like exercises in obedience to the aliens that have kidnapped the bottom.

In virtual real-time, the top and bottom are connected by modem, and write back and forth; this can also be done as phone sex. It is assumed that both or all partners may be masturbating throughout, and the top may give specific instruction on how to do that, or interrupt the bottom to make him or her wait, or forbid an orgasm (yet), or whatever other means of exercising control intrigue the fertile mind.

The advantages of virtual S/M lie in anonymity. Comfortably ensconced in your home, you can present yourself as any being in your fantasies, and see who responds to you, and how. You can get to know people before you may choose to meet them - some players use cyberspace as a way to find people to play with in the real world, and others do virtual play for its own sake. Computer communication also offers an excellent venue for negotiating real-world scenes, faster than mail but more comprehensive and less embarrassing than face-to-face or phone conversations.

We think you should plan and negotiate scenes by computer with as much care as you would to play in person. A person's limits might be different in virtual reality than they are in real life, but most people find that they do indeed have limits, and that virtual play can be both as exciting and as upsetting as playing in person.

Virtual players like to rise to the challenge of finding words to describe the unspeakable, and virtual sex is much like writing erotica. The text usually includes lengthy and evocative descriptions not only of physical acts but also of the feelings, physical and emotional, they have in response to those acts, paced to give people time to get turned on, to get into each phase of the experience, and ultimately to get off.

Full-Time S/M

Some players live in their S/M roles full-time: Master or Mistress and slave, or Daddy and boy, Mommy and girl, Mistress and dog, houseboy or French maid. In some people's eyes, living full-time is the ultimate expression of S/M, complete immersion in the fantasy, making the fantasy their total reality.

Sometimes elaborate S/M families are formed, where a senior top's girl might have a slave of her own, and another human may be functioning as the dog. Players form these families according to their needs, and demonstrate a startling facility to adapt to changing conditions — there's no rule that says you can't make agreements to change roles in whatever way suits you.

And for those who are successful, wonderfully fulfilling and creative lives can follow. We would like to point out that living full-time in role is not for everyone - among other things, it seems to increase the difficulty of maintaing safe boundaries between fantasy and reality - and those who practice their S/M in scene and drop roles at other times are in no way inferior.

Living in a full-time S/M relationship has its rewards and its pitfalls. The reward is the opportunity to delve into your S/M self with tremendous intensity and manifest your top or bottom persona in a very complete way.

Contracts. There are many ways to do full-time S/M relationships, and one way that people get clear about what they are doing is to write a contract, often called a slave or ownership contract, in which the rights and responsibilities of both parties are spelled out. Why a contract? You might think that when you own someone they just do what you want all the time. Well, there are always limits, and if your bottom's limits offend you, remember that you probably have limits of your own. For instance, when you own a slave, does that mean you have to be lean and mean and in top role twenty-four hours a day, or do you get to relax now and then? If you have a little boy or girl in an adult body, do you have to get up in the middle of the night when s/he has bad dreams? Are you contracting to provide income for both of you, or who goes to work and how do they do it? Contracts also normally cover agreements about monogamy and nonmonogamy: are both parties monogamous? If not, what are their responsibilities to each other? Can the top give the slave away to someone else? Can the slave ask to be given to someone else?

There are many creative ways to accomplish communication in role without resorting to manipulation. One Mistress of our acquaintance has her slave write a journal entry onto the computer every morning, with orders to include information about his state of well-being, his emotional reality and any problems he might be experiencing. She can then read what he wrote, and decide on her response, without breaking role unless she chooses to.

Lifestyle play has generated many clever devices to keep the bottom enslaved when the top is not present. You can padlock a chain around his waist, or give her instructions to go into the bathroom at work at two o'clock and masturbate for five minutes without coming, and so on...

If people owning slaves or otherwise involved in relationships with a declared power inequity push your buttons, please remember that these lifestyles were consciously chosen, which may put them a step ahead of traditional marriages and the power dynamics of traditional sex roles that most people don't even think about. And role-bound relationships work well for a lot of people. Many people are relieved to have a clear idea about who is empowered to do, say or decide what, and many bottoms are quite content to let their masters or mistresses run the show.

We observe that people who do well at lifestyle relationship usually have very clear boundaries, even if they don't call them that, and can readily describe how they know when they are in and out of role, or which roles, or how deeply. They tend to be good at signals, and slide in and out of role with facility. They have respect for everybody's roles, bottoms and tops alike, and take pride in playing their part well.

Public Play

The play party has become a basic institution in many S/M communities, so basic that we have been asked if a person can explore S/M at all if s/he doesn't want to play in public. Of course you can play without going to play parties, and many do. But public play is very popular among S/M players, so if you have fantasies of large audiences applauding and cheering your amazing sexual feats, we have a party for you.

Play parties are usually held in a space designed for that purpose, possibly a dungeon in someone's home, or the studio of a professional dominant. Other party play spaces are maintained by support groups as a volunteer endeavor, and some people make a profession of running a party house. Some clubs in major cities are set up for public S/M play, some on one night a week, some all the time. A play party space usually will have one or more dungeons equipped with furniture - one or more slings, a St. Andrew's cross, medical examination tables, bondage tables, overhead hoists, cages, and the like... occasionally even beds. Conversation in the play area is discouraged because it intrudes on the consciousness of the people who are playing.

Normally there is also a social area, where food and beverages are available, where people can meet and cruise and negotiate, or come down after a scene. Most party houses have a set of rules or guidelines printed up for you, covering their expectations about everything from safe sex to responsible voyeurism, and most have dungeon monitors on duty throughout the party so there is always someone who can answer your questions. Safety is a prominent concern - what a nightmare to have to call an ambulance in the middle of an S/M orgy!

The play party provides a safe opportunity to meet people, watch how they play, explore new partners and play in a playful environment, with not so much personal commitment beyond the moment. Some monogamous couples come to watch others, socialize and to play special scenes for public display - we like to watch these scenes because couples who have played together for a long time are often very good at it, and you can see the intimacy and profound connection. People who like to watch are asked to be responsible, and keep at a non-intrusive distance. We enjoy voyeurism a lot - we get the chance to learn from what other people do, and tons of ideas and how-tos to take back to our own play. The encouragement of an eager audience helps many people push their limits - be careful not to let the crowd's enthusiasm push you into doing something you'll regret later, though.

Seeing others play can also help us feel more okay about ourselves. Dossie says: "When I see someone very turned on, stark naked and thrashing and looking real good, and that person is not necessarily young or thin, then I start to realize that maybe I look good when I play even if I'm not built like a centerfold. And when I see other tops taking their time, dealing with the equipment and their bottoms, going through all the effort and technical work to get a scene off the ground, and then I see that scene flying into the stratosphere, that helps me not feel like an idiot when it takes me a little time to get a scene working."

We also like the challenge of play parties. When we prepare a scene for a play party, we often put in extra effort to make something that will be powerful for us and attact an appreciative audience, and playing in public gives an edge to a scene that can help it go further, or higher, or wherever you want it to go.

We believe that the deprivatization of sex is a radical political act. Hush-hush attitudes toward sex have generated a sick history of shame, embarrassment, guilt and self-loathing that have crippled many people - kept them from realizing their wonderful sexual selves and often decimated their entire sense of self-esteem. In S/M in particular, coming out is often made difficult by feelings of shame and inadequacy, as well as the problem of acquiring the extensive technical information and experience that make a good top or bottom. All of these difficulties can be addressed at the play party, where the opportunity to share sex and S/M with others can be powerfully healing, where you can stand up in public and do yourself - and your bottom - proud.

14. Shadow Play: Darkside S/M

What Is It?

Shadow play is our name for scenes that delve into deep psychological issues. It is our understanding that all S/M involves explorations of parts of ourselves that we may have tucked away in that immense mental storehouse that Jung called the Shadow. As you learn your emotional limits in S/M, you may find yourself wanting to push those limits by deliberately setting up an S/M scene to travel in forbidden territory, to delve into emotions like rage or misery that can cause dysfunction if allowed to run free in our real lives. Playing in parent/child roles is often deep play, as is playing out personal trauma like child abuse, molestation or rape. Some players may use an S/M scene to explore historical social oppression, like slavery, witch-burnings, the Inquisition or the Holocaust.

Dossie had a powerful experience of reclaiming a piece of her history after the scene with Catherine that we told you about before, where Dossie was a poor waif in a Victorian workhouse. She recalls:

> Catherine had cleverly gotten around my limit about playing with punishment by caning me "to show you what would happen if you ever did do something you shouldn't." My role required nothing of me but to whimper and be pathetic for about three hours, a feeling I found to be curiously luxurious. Wondering about this the next day brought to mind a time in my life when I really was pathetic – in my early twenties I had to leave a violent partner when I was pregnant, with just about no resources. I used to hang

out at this ecumenical ministry in the Haight because they gave me free yogurt, which for a few weeks was my primary source of protein. I'm sure I looked pretty pathetic to them, but that's not how I felt about myself: I was angry at myself, blaming myself for having gotten into this situation in the first place, and I was determined to be strong enough to pull my life back together, which I did. It took an S/M scene 25 years later to bring me to compassion for myself and permission to give myself some comfort, which I found very healing. Now when I remember that time in my life I no longer feel ashamed.

The charge that each of us as individuals may have on a particular scenario is what makes it deep. Many of us play rape scenes, and more than a few of us have actually been raped, so for some a rape scene is very deep play, searching for understanding, catharsis, healing or resolution.

Play can be deep for the top or the bottom or both. If we re-enact a scene of abuse, it is not only the bottom who may be playing deep. Survivors of child abuse frequently carry with them what they learned from the adults, engraved into their psyches as the internalized abuser. Tops may experience profound emotion in playing the role of bully or punitive parent.

Many people are attracted to playing in their shadows because it is very hot, intriguing, sexy. This might be the same desire that could lead us to re-enact the same dysfunction over and over in our relationship, or repeatedly pick the partner who makes us the craziest. Dossie used to express this desire by hunting down rough trade in the streets of New York (she found lots of it, too); Catherine used to have such a profound need to be needed that she drove herself and her partners crazy by insisting that they need her even when they didn't. We find it a lot safer and more constructive to play out our old tapes within the boundaries of an S/M scene. We can relive our old dramas to our heart's content, only this time we control the outcome. In this lies empowerment, with great potential for healing and transformation.

140

Deep Emotional Safety

In a previous chapter we told you how to handle psychological emergencies that might come up when your play accidentally sets off somebody's emotional land mines. In shadow play, you go into that same territory on purpose, and these skills will be your safety net, enabling you to get back out whenever you want to, no matter how deeply you have gone in. This is advanced play, and we do not advocate shadow play with new partners or with unfamiliar physical techniques - this is no time to fumble. And let us remind you that just as we deplore S/M values that add up to a hierarchy of hip about heaviness in stimulus play, there is no status value in playing deeper than the next guy - play at the depth that feels right to you.

There are still limits, there are always limits - but it may be trickier figuring out what they are. Both of us, for example, have limits about face-slapping because our parents used to do that, so we only allow face-slapping in scenes that are planned to be deep. Catherine tells potential tops, "If you slap my face I may come unglued; don't do it unless you're willing to help put me back together again." Punishment for real or imagined naughtiness may be hot for one player, too sensitive for another. You may discover a limit you didn't know you had. Dossie remembers:

My partner had been playing Mommy to my very young baby, personae that we had fooled around with while snuggling, but never in an actual S/M scene. When we discussed playing a scene with the baby, we decided that it was too scary to hurt her, but that sex might be okay. In scene, I got deeply into my baby role, being fed ice cream, playing with toys, sucking on everything. When we progressed to the sexual part, though, I got confused, overwhelmed and profoundly disturbed. I began to cry in a strange and mournful way, and my partner stopped the sex and comforted me. What I got from the scene was that the baby was not big enough to have sex, and that, since my family was very stern and intolerant of crying children, it was

141

incredibly healing to be comforted when I was upset, with no justifications needed. So in one way this scene was a disaster, and in another way it was a healing experience. (In case you were worried, the baby is fine and just learned to say "doggie.")

When you play with emotional risk, plan to spend some time talking about feelings. Honor your feelings, whatever they may be, as the scene reveals them to you - there is no way that you are "supposed" to feel.

Also remember that you already have psychological defenses that have been protecting you from your own painful stuff. S/M technique may bypass these defenses for the duration of the scene, but will not disable them. Your normal defenses will return in due time and continue to protect you as well as they always have. Above all, stay conscious and honor the fragility with which you are playing. Shadow play requires a commitment from all players to serious exploration, and a willingness to give that exploration the time, energy and respect it deserves.

How Do You Do It?

Beginning. So you have inklings of some part of yourself that you or your partner wants to explore. The next question becomes: how do you get there? If you discovered this space in play by accident, then once you have established some safety nets, you can return by the same route that got you there in the first place: a role, a script, a costume, a phrase, a whipping or whatever. You might be surprised to find it less scary this time - when you make the choice to walk a risky path, you are much more in control, and it's amazing what the light of consciousness can do to defuse old fears.

You may already have a script in mind, an old fantasy, something you read that turns you on. A lot of S/M erotica has the primal intensity of myth, because fantasies often express the dynamics that run our unconscious minds.

You can approach psychological depths by going through old wounds, re-enacting abuse, becoming parent, child, perpetrator, bully, brat, crybaby and vicious schoolmarm. You can act out forbidden feelings - angry, guilty, mean - and their equally forbidden opposites, pathetic, needy, frightened, ashamed. Find the feelings that are most powerful for you by going for the juice, the charge, the place where your emotions are strong and scary: this is your fire. You built your fireplace when you negotiated your scene, so you are safe, and you can explore one step at a time - leaping into abysses is optional. To increase the intensity, you can make heat with friction, rubbing together or pushing against each other to amplify, blow up flames from coals.

Middle. What do you do when you get into those intense roles and feelings? Let your physical script support you. For instance, if you and your bottom have agreed on a flogging, as the heat rises you can imagine running your intense feelings down your arm and out the end of the whip into your bottom - believe us, s/he will feel it, and you will too.

You can use any activity as a focus for your energy, and to get more fully into your role. Know your bottom: limits, preferences, what gets the endorphins running, what arouses, what triggers an orgasm.

Who says you have to be consistent? Tops can play from multiple positions in the same scene, from torture, wickedness and betrayal to support, love and nurturance. The inquisitor who tortures the sinner must have great love to go to such lengths to save that immortal soul, right? Techniques of interrogation can be used to confuse and liberate the bottom by generating a double-bind, like ordering someone to tell the truth as you insist that s/he lie, just like real brainwashing. For betrayal, you can make your bottom struggle to meet your demands and then punish him or her for succeeding. The ways to create no-win situations for mindfuck are endless, and most of them are based on intensely polarized contrast between hurting and caressing. We see no contradiction in a big bad mean top who has just tortured some poor bottom, now patting that bottom on the back while murmuring "there, there, poor baby, you're all right now."

We empower ourselves when we replay old scripts and arrange for them to come out differently. Ideally, all S/M scenes end in a win for both players. Orgasm is a good win for just about everybody, and orgasm is not the only way to win. The successful completion of a scene gives feelings of competence, mastery, control and empowerment, and as the top you can reinforce those feelings in your bottom by offering praise for how well s/he took the sensations, or by letting your bottom know how good you feel, how turned on you are. S/he can tell you how wonderful you are too.

Most of what we dig up from our shadows consists of feelings or roles that we have some shame about, so sharing that piece of ourselves is powerfully intimate. We are letting another person into a part of ourselves that we ourselves may have rejected. And when that person accepts us, complete with our old tapes, and responds with erotic enthusiasm, then we get the ultimate validation: love given to the part of ourselves that we may fear most.

Ending. You close a deep scene just as you close any other scene, only make sure you do it. Don't skimp on time and energy for the return trip to the so-called real world. When you prepare for voyaging in the shadows, discuss how much time you will have afterwards, if anyone thinks s/he may want time alone, if you will sleep together, whatever feels most comfortable. Do allow lots of time for snuggling and good feelings, and do check back in over the next several days so you both can talk about any aftershocks you may experience.

What About Therapy?

Does deep psychological play make the top into a therapist? Emphatically no. Shadow play can be therapeutic, and indeed healing, but is very different from a therapeutic relationship. Ideally, your relationship with a professional therapist is an island where you can explore your inner truth with no consequences in the rest of your life. An S/M scene is also an island, but with very different rules and boundaries. If you find yourself digging up a profound conflict, maybe in the form of

145

intense emotions, panicky feelings or flashbacks to old trauma, you might well want to seek therapy, whether or not you plan to play with this dynamic in S/M. When an old conflict opens up, there is opportunity for healing, and therapy will not only protect your partner from having to be your therapist, but will allow you to work on your issues at a time that is very likely to be profitable for you. In the Resource Guide, you will find an address to write to for a listing of S/M-friendly therapists.

Shadows and Rebirth

There is a Native American medicine story about Crow who dances between the worlds. At one time Crow became fascinated with her shadow. She could not leave it alone. She kept looking at it, scratching it, poking at it, pecking it, until her shadow woke up and came to life. Then Crow's shadow ate her.

In this story, Crow gets chewed up to emerge transformed, with the ability to travel in other dimensions. Many myths feature heroes and heroines who travel into the shadows, get destroyed and then reborn, transformed and enlightened by the experience. These stories warn that travel in the shadow is both dangerous and rewarding. We have written here what we know about how to travel as safely as possible in your precious darkness. If your intuition tells you that this kind of play does not feel safe or growthful to you, we suggest that you trust your inner wisdom and refrain. Perhaps later you may feel different, and perhaps you will not. Perhaps another path will work better for your journey to self-knowledge.

Once again, all S/M play is shadow play - when we do S/M, we find acceptance for emotions and behaviors that would be unacceptable outside scene space. And we believe that all S/M is potentially, and potently, healing and growthful.

When we venture purposefully into our darkest shadows, we get to write our own script, determine the outcome, validate forbidden and rejected parts of ourselves, reclaim parts of ourselves that we had lost or buried, and find ways to grasp all the parts of ourselves, every single one, in a profound act of self-acceptance through which we may become whole.

146

15. S/M Spirituality: From the Top

Sex is spiritual. We live in a culture that has historically insisted that sex and spirituality are mutually exclusive, in a country founded by puritans who were convinced that God hates sex. But as radical perverts, our experience and our belief is that sex *is* spiritual, and that a simple honest orgasm is a spiritual experience.

Sexuality has been a path for both of us - the road we originally took to question our individual and social programming. Discovering the ways in which we as women could grasp our sexuality was a powerful way to heal from our childhoods and from our sex-negative culture. We have proceeded from that healing to further self-exploration, and ultimately to celebrating our spirituality in the practice of S/M.

It has been pointed out that you can tell we are living in a sex-negative culture by the way we talk about sexuality as if it were an object, a thing with distinct boundaries that we can separate from the rest of our experience. We believe that if we truly accepted our sexuality, we would understand that sexual energy flows through everything all the time, like spiritual energy, like the life force, like the Tao, like a river. The cosmic river flows through each of us, bearing nourishment, washing away what we no longer need, making us wet. With S/M as our boat, we can travel on that river to and beyond our wildest dreams.

Shadow and Spirit

On the next page is a grossly oversimplified diagram of how psychologist Carl Jung viewed the human psyche, modeling

147

spirituality as both a personal and a universal awareness that he called the Collective Unconscious. We told you before about the shadow, that dark and scary reservoir of everything we have decided to banish from our awareness. We explained how we use S/M to explore our darkness, illuminate it with our clear awareness, and reclaim forbidden territory as psychological healing, a way of becoming whole. And all of this is spiritual.

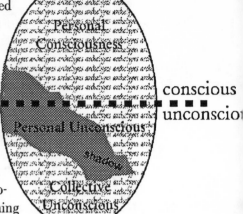

When we add ritual to our S/M, performing it with spiritual intention, we can travel deeper yet... beyond the personal unconscious mind and into universal consciousness, or spiritual awareness. So the shadow, our personal garbage pit, becomes the gateway through which we pass to travel in realms beyond ordi-nary consciousness, like Crow who dances between the worlds.

S/M Ritual as Spiritual Path

Ritual S/M is edge play directed to the purpose of attaining altered states of consciousness, of traveling beyond our habitual perceptual screens to another way of being in which everything becomes special, extraordinary, brilliant. Goals for such a scene might be a quest for guidance or a vision, the pursuit of personal truth and understanding, or the experience of spiritual communion for its own sake.

S/M players have devised rituals for these purposes by mixing our sexual exploration and our own personal mythologies (our S/M roles and stories, like The Kidnapping of the Pleasure Slave) with spiritual practices we learn from other traditions: kundalini yoga, the rites of Kali, vision quest, wherever we find the images that help us manifest what is beyond our ability to imagine. Take, for example, a scene based on the simple act of chanting. Dossie recalls:

My bottom and I were in deep grief over a mutual friend and mentor we had lost to AIDS, and we had decided to seek release in ritual S/M. I tied her to a padded table and flogged her to the point of weeping, all the while chanting "Om Krim Kalyae Namaha," an invocation to Kali, the terrifying Hindu goddess of death and birth. As I struck with the whip in rhythm with the chant, I felt myself go into trance, the words of the chant serving to occupy my conscious mind, leaving me free to feel the energy flowing through the whip, my bottom's grief surging beneath me, until I felt in myself Kali the inexorable, the implacable force of nature which dictates that everything we love must die. My partner struggled with her grief, writhing and thrashing, held safe by the bondage, and wept copiously, chanting "Jaia Ma," an invocation to the Mother goddess, over and over, until both of our grief and despair had been fully poured out, and we had reached a sense of exhausted peace with the universe. The Hindus say of Kali that there is no way to understand her, no logic to explain her, no justification – she is like a storm, we have no choice but to love her, and in that love, come to acceptance of our human condition.

Edge play. The edge in edge play is found wherever your edge is, wherever things start to feel risky, where you start to feel vulnerable, the edge of the cliff that looks over your personal abyss. Playing on the edge challenges the top into heightened awareness. A bondage top of our acquaintance specializes in rope suspension, the art of hanging a bottom in mid-air supported by nothing but rope. The challenge of playing on the edge of her skill and knowledge brings her into her top space, and awakens her psychic and spiritual power. Sometimes she has visions and sees animal spirits. She sees her task as to open and balance the body so the spirit - kundalini energy - can flow through freely. When the bondage sends the bottom flying, sex may have a place as a grounding sensation, bringing the person back into his or her body in a state of bliss.

In the balance of bondage, we play with suspension, with suspense, with gravity, with the energy of the entire planet.[1]

Let us not forget that ordinary consciousness is really extraordinary too, a miracle whose workings we have not even begun to fathom. Even our defenses, that we complain about when we have difficulty opening up, should be honored, because they form the skin that protects and contains us. Our ego is both our mask and our means of communication, how we define the boundaries between ourselves and the person beside us. So honor your defenses, your shell, your mask, even when you are in the process of putting them aside. Thank them for protecting you.

People experience spirituality in many different ways, and all of them are valid. It has been said that any path, walked with mindfulness and honesty, can lead to enlightenment. What different descriptions of spiritual awakening often have in common is the feeling of casting off everyday consciousness and opening to beautiful, potent energy from inside or outside yourself. S/M has the power to open up perceptions so that you can see more than you usually do, become hyperconscious.

Roles in ritual. To top in ritual S/M, you need to be a responsible guide. You need to train yourself, develop your own spiritual practice, and educate yourself far beyond what you can learn from reading this one chapter in this one small book. You must be ready to care for your bottom, to operate from your own most serious wisdom, to trust and honor your bottom's wisdom, and always to empower your bottom. To use ritual to aggrandize yourself or to bolster your flagging ego by belittling your bottom is unethical, and a violation of sacred space.

When both people in a ritual let their masks down they recognize one another in a way that permits validation of all the parts of themselves. They may express those parts as personae they have discovered through the archetypes, the

---

1. *Special thanks to Kaye Buckley for her observations and insight.*

images of the divine manifest in human form that we call gods and goddesses - or they may simply feel what is absolutely real, needing no further definition.

Start by knowing yourself, and knowing your intention. Be clean in your intentions, and keep the boundaries clear and clean. Respect that the bottom is allowing you to come into his or her most precious places, opening up to allow you deeper contact, contributing spirit and courage to this journey.

S/M ritual requires *mutual* openness, which means that you, the top, must also be willing to expose yourself, to get vulnerable, to make connection. It is possible to open a bottom's psyche up with good ritual technique, but to pour yourself into him or her when s/he is open requires that you be open too. When you open the energy in yourself it becomes a light by which you can find that energy in another. You put yourself in a position that requires empathy and psychic connection, and so you are more likely to find it.

The top starts out as a caretaker, and that task and the empathy it requires can open up the dance for you. When we set out to guide another toward spiritual truth, we must consciously grasp our own wisdom: in a way, our wisdom is not complete until we share it with another. The skilled top becomes the shaman, the dramaturge, the spirit guide, the magician who pulls down energy from the cosmos and opens pathways to expanded awareness. The bottom contributes to and shares in that energy as you send him or her out spinning into personal visions, while you, as top, get to ride your bottom's energy and discover yet more of your own potential, your potency, your power. When we see our spirit reflected in the magic mirror of our bottom's glowing eyes, we become free to realize the god/dess within both of us.

Ritual Practice

So how do you make an S/M scene into a ritual? A ritual is the performance of a series of symbolic acts that act like keys to change our state of awareness. To do ritual successfully, we begin by creating a sacred space, a place free of interruptions or everyday constraints, a safe space of mutual trust and respect, an optimum space to focus on the journeying. We clear the everyday stuff out of the way so we can feel the subtler energy of spiritual consciousness.

Start with cleansing both of you, individually or together. A bath scented with fresh lemons or a bubble bath will do fine - it's the attention you focus on the cleansing that achieves it. Imagine washing all the tension off and letting it gurgle down the drain. Let your attention travel over your entire body, feeling how the warm water relaxes each part, allowing vibrant energy to fill you up. Visualize each little attachment dissolving and flowing into the sea.

Pack up all your cares and woes... try writing them on a piece of paper and putting the paper in your freezer for a time. Respect your cares by promising them that you will return to pick them up again when your ritual is over. They may be different by then.

Cleanse the space, the room in which you will play out your ritual. Sweep, dust, remove dissonant objects, bring in fresh sheets and towels, sweeten the air with herbs or incense. Perform these humble acts with all the consciousness you can bring to them.

Create a focus in the space, a setting for your journey, with candles, music, pillows to nestle in, perhaps an altar of objects that carry special significance. In time you may develop your own symbol system - images and stories, deities, crystals, bones, whatever resonates for you - your personal symbol structure is your web of connection with the flow of nature and the divine, keys that open the doors to heightened states of consciousness.

In ritual space, choose carefully who and what you allow close to you - when your mask is off, you are both more open and more vulnerable. As we cleanse and protect our sacred space, we build a safe hearth to contain some very wild fires.

Planning and negotiating. Rituals get negotiated just like any other scene, by talking about what is important to each of

152

you, preparing to validate and respect everyone's limits. An S/M ritual may or may not incorporate genital sex. It may or may not incorporate pain. It may or may not include opening the skin. You can ritualize anything by doing it with intention, and you give a special significance to instruments that you employ in ritual. So clean all your toys too.

The physical focus of a ritual might be a flogging, or other intense stimulus to raise endorphins. Bondage can be ritual in and of itself, a meditation on rope and constraint, muscles and limbs, balance. You can open the skin with piercings or cutting, for the sensation of it, to imprint a mark of symbolic meaning, or to connect through that opening.

Good ritual has a beginning, a middle and an end. It starts by defining where you are, by cleaning and by forming a circle or enclosed psychic space, and by defining your intention - perhaps with an invocation to whatever deity has relevance to your purpose. In the middle you perform the acts you have agreed upon, and see where they take you. The end is closure, in which you return to normal consciousness, often by going back over the symbolic path that you walked in the beginning, thanking the powers and deities on the way, and returning any energy you may have raised that you can no longer use.

Ritual *works*. Symbolic acts have real consequences in our lives, the power of pulling down energy to manifest in the real world, of bringing spirit into our bodies and onto the planet, of *realizing*. It is dangerous to treat ritual frivolously. Have respect.

Power and Manifestation

We are using the metaphors of power and cosmic energy interchangeably, because our understanding is that personal power *is* the universal life force, power that we can access whether we envision it as coming from within or from outside us. Catherine, when a scene is working well, feels energy from some external source pour into her like white light - others report seeing that light in her too. When this is happening, she feels as if she can do no wrong, that she is totally connected to

153

what she is doing with her bottom. Dossie feels the energy welling up from within herself, or perhaps from underneath her, earth power from Her hot molten interior, and when that power is with her she also feels totally empowered and in total communication with her bottom.

With that power, personal, cosmic, planetary, comes the understanding that we are all manifestations of the same thing, and that we have the power to change how we manifest ourselves. This is the power of transformation, and of transcendence. To manifest is to realize, to make real and thereby understand. In S/M we take a fantasy, a myth, a vision or a dream and manifest it, live it out in our bodies, bring it into the material world and sculpt with the forces of endorphins, eroticism and consciousness.

15. The Light that Shines in the Darkness

Who tells me Thou art dark
Oh my Mother divine?
Thousands of suns and moons
From Thy body do shine!
— *translation of a Hindu chant to Kali*[1]

We sadomasochists are always playing out heroic myths, and exploring altered awareness. What lies beyond the edge, over the cliff? The journey leads into darkness, into the unknown, where we must walk with care because we cannot see our footing, like exploring in caves deep under the earth. Thus, all S/M is to some degree ritual - a voyage of self-discovery, a journey through the darkness and toward the light of transcendence.

The darkness may be of our own creating, but we still cannot see what is in there until we are courageous enough to enter it. Then it is our own consciousness that becomes the light that shines in the darkness, that illuminates our inner landscape as if we carried spotlights in our metaphysical (or metaphorical) eyes.

The archangel of the territory of the Earth is Lucifer, often pictured as a frightening goatish demon of evil and darkness. But in the Cabala, the name Lucifer actually means lightbearer; he is the fallen angel who goes into unfathomable darkness with an unquenchable light inside him, and who carries the power of the villain and of the emancipator.

---

1.   From *"May Thy Light Shine Forever,"* audiotape, *Crystal Clarity Publishers, Nevada City, CA.*

It is within the darkness of the earth, in the cool depths where seeds germinate, that the material of waste and decay is transformed into fertilizer for new life. When we evoke our personal demons in an S/M scene, we dig up the darkest and most difficult aspects of life's journey, and with the magic of erotic energy transform that shit into our rose garden.

S/M is sex magic, and you are the magician. The bottom is the cauldron in which you perform your miracles. Wave your wand, and make magic happen... as you mix your bottom's power and your own, heat them up with the fire of passion, and with that potent precious power turn lead into gold, misery into exaltation, bondage into liberation and sex into revelation.

So have a great journey, with our blessings - and more power to you.

Catherine A. Liszt   Dossie Easton

March, 1996

Resource Guide

This was a difficult section to compile, as there are so many excellent resources. We picked a few of the oldest and best-known, and a few of our personal favorites - but there are hundreds of great ones we didn't have room for.

Gateway Resources

These resources can open doors to a vast number of people, clubs, publications and ideas: hence, we call them "gateways."

San Francisco Sex Information
(415) 621-7374
A hot line staffed with trained and knowledgeable volunteers who can answer your S/M and sexuality questions, or guide you toward someone who can.

Black Book
P.O. Box 31155
San Francisco, CA   94131
http://www.queernet.org/BlackBooks
An international compendium of resources for various sexual minorities, particularly leatherfolk. Published annually.

Good Vibrations
mail-order: 938 Howard St. #101
retail: 1210 Valencia St., San Francisco
             San Francisco, CA 94103
             (800) 974-8989
e-mail goodvibe@well.com
http://www.goodvibes.com

Not specifically an S/M store, but a wonderful source for books and toys of all kinds.

QSM
P.O. Box 882242
San Francisco, CA 94188-2242
(415) 550-7776
http://www.qualitysm.com
A huge mail-order collection of S/M literature, including books, magazines and newspapers. Also puts on S/M workshops from entry-level through advanced.

Kink-Aware Professionals
c/o Race Bannon
584 Castro Street #518
San Francisco, CA 94114-2500
e-mail: 72114.2327@compuserve.com
http://www.bannon.com/~race/kap
Race Bannon, author of "Learning the Ropes," has compiled a nationwide listing of therapists, physicians and other professionals who have understanding and sympathy for sexual minorities. Send him a business-sized SASE with two regular stamps on it to receive a copy of the list.

Clubs

It is impossible to maintain an up-to-the-minute listing of S/M clubs - they appear and disappear on an almost daily basis. Still, here are some of the largest and best established ones nationwide.

National Leather Association *(pansexual, many chapters)*
3439 North East Sandy Blvd. #155
Portland, OR 97232
(614) 470-2093

Chicago Hellfire Club *(men)*
P.O. Box 5426
Chicago, IL 60680

Chicagoland Discussion Group *(pansexual)*
P.O. Box 25009
Chicago, IL   60625
http://www.angelfire.com/pages0/CDG/index.html

The Eulenspiegel Society *(pansexual)*
P.O. Box 2783
New York, NY   10163-2783
(212) 633-8376
http://www.tes.org

GMSMA (Gay Male SM Activists) *(men)*
332 Bleecker St. #D23
New York, NY   10014
(212) 727-9878
http://www.ability.net/gmsma

LSM (Lesbian Sex Mafia) *(women)*
P.O. Box 993
Murray Hill Station
New York, NY   10156

Outcasts *(women)*
P.O. Box 31266
San Francisco, CA   94131

The Society of Janus *(pansexual)*
P.O. Box 426795
San Francisco, CA 94142
(415) 985-7117
http://www.soj.com

Threshold *(pansexual)*
2554 Lincoln Blvd. #1004
Marina Del Rey, CA   90291

Magazines and Newspapers

Again, S/M publications change as quickly as the weather.
Still, here are some that have been around for a while,
spreading the good word:

Bad Attitude *(lesbian)*
P.O. Box 39110
Cambridge, MA   02139

Kinky People, Places and Things *(heterosexual)*
P.O. Box 10515
Seattle, WA   98189

Black Sheets *(pansexual)*
P.O. Box 31155
San Francisco, CA   94131

Boudoir Noir *(pansexual)*
P.O. Box 5, Stn. F
Toronto, ON
Canada M4Y 2L4
(416) 591-2387
http://www.boudoir-noir.com

Brat Attack *(lesbian - published by our illustrator Fish)*
P.O. Box 40754
San Francisco, CA   94141-0754

CuirUnderground *(pansexual)*
3288 21st St. #19
San Francisco, CA   94110
http://www.black-rose.com/cuiru.html

Drummer *(gay male)*
P.O. Box 410390
San Francisco, CA   94141-0390

Greenery: Lady Green's Newsletter for Women & Men Exploring Female Domination
3739 Balboa Ave. #195
San Francisco, CA 94121

Prometheus *(Eulenspiegel Society newsletter; pansexual)*
P.O. Box 2783
New York, NY   10163-2783
http://www.tes.org

Sandmutopian Guardian *(pansexual)*
P.O. Box 1146
New York, NY   10156

Books

We obviously think very highly of the books published by our publisher Greenery Press, which are listed on the back page of this book. Here are some others we like:

The Complete Guide to Safer Sex, *edited by the Instute for Advanced Study of Human Sexuality*
Barricade Books, Fort Lee, NJ

Different Loving: An Exploration of the World of Sexual Dominance and Submission, *by Brame, Brame and Jacobs*
Villard Books, New York

The Good Vibrations Guide to Sex, *by Cathy Winks and Ann Semans*
Down There Press, San Francisco

Exhibitionism for the Shy, *by Carol Queen*
Down There Press, San Francisco

Consensual Sadomasochism: How to Talk About It and How to Do It Safely, *by William A. Henkin, Ph.D. and Sybil Holiday, CCSSE*
Daedalus Publishing Co., San Francisco

Learning the Ropes, *by Race Bannon*
Daedalus Publishing Co., San Francisco

Leatherfolk, *edited by Mark Thompson*
Alyson Publications, Boston

The Lesbian S/M Safety Manual, *edited by Pat Califia*
Alyson Publications, Boston

The Loving Dominant, *by John Warren*
Masquerade Books, New York

My Private Life: Real Experiences of a Dominant Woman, *by Mistress Nan*
Daedalus Publishing Co., San Francisco

Safe, Sane, Consensual - And Fun, *by John Warren*
Diversified Services, Brighton, MA

Screw the Roses, Send Me the Thorns, *by Philip Miller &
Molly Devon*
Mystic Rose Books, Fairfield, CT

Sensuous Magic, *by Pat Califia*
Masquerade Books, New York

**Ties That Bind: The SM/Leather/Fetish Erotic Style -
Issues, Commentaries and Advice**, *by Guy Baldwin*
Daedalus Publishing, San Francisco

Electronic Resources

The Internet newsgroups alt.sex.bondage, alt.sex.femdom
and alt.sex.spanking, among others, offer advice, ideas,
fiction and contacts. There are also many private electronic
mailing lists, notably gl-asb (gay & lesbian alt.sex.bondage),
offered on the 'Net itself and by various on-line providers.
In addition, many local BBSs (computer bulletin boards)
specialize in various sexual alternatives, including S/M.

Scream

from lungs that fill your whole body
    Scream
because you can't keep it in and you won't let it out
    Scream
the storm that blows ocean through you, wind,
smoke
    Scream
so huge I have to suck in air to help

I love your scream
    because you scream tears into my eyes
I love your scream
    because it howls through all your beautiful
holes
I love your scream
    because of everybody who has ever screamed

Scream into my mouth
Scream into my cunt
Scream into my clever hands
Scream into this poem

Lover, if you suffer for me
    Scream for me

- Lady Green

Other Publications from Greenery Press

The Bottoming Book: Or, How To Get Terrible Things Done To You By Wonderful People
Dossie Easton & Catherine A. Liszt, illustrated by Fish $11.95

The Compleat Spanker
Lady Green $11.95

A Hand in the Bush: The Fine Art of Vaginal Fisting
Deborah Addington $11.95

KinkyCrafts: 101 Do-It-Yourself S/M Toys
compiled and edited by Lady Green with Jaymes Easton $19.95

Mercy??! No!!!
Kinky cartoons by B.N. Duncan $9.95

Miss Abernathy's Concise Slave Training Manual
Christine Abernathy $11.95

Sex Toy Tricks: More than 125 Ways to Accessorize Good Sex
Jay Wiseman $11.95

The Sexually Dominant Woman: A Workbook for Nervous Beginners
Lady Green $11.95

SM 101: A Realistic Introduction - 2nd Edition
Jay Wiseman $24.95

Supermarket Tricks: More than 125 Ways to Improvise Good Sex
Jay Wiseman $11.95

Tricks: More than 125 Ways to Make Good Sex Better
Jay Wiseman $11.95

Tricks 2: _Another_ 125 Ways to Make Good Sex Better
Jay Wiseman $11.95

Coming in 1997

The Ethical Slut, by Dossie Easton and Catherine A. Liszt

Bottom Lines, spanking verses by Algernon H. Swinbume

The Origins of Sadomasochism, the posthumous masterpiece of Donald Miesen

*Please include $3 for first book and $1 each for each additional book with your order
to cover shipping and handling costs. VISA/MC accepted. Order from:*

Greenery
Press

3739 Balboa Ave. #195, San Francisco, CA 94121
http://www.bigrock.coml-greenery